# The North Pennines landscape

A landscape assessment
prepared by Land Use Consultants
for the Countryside Commission

Published by:
Countryside Commission
John Dower House
Crescent Place
Cheltenham GL50 3RA
© Countryside Commission 1991

Distributed by:
Countryside Commission Publications
19/23 Albert Road
Manchester M19 2EQ
CCP 318
Price £7.00

2

# Contents

# Figures

**British Library Cataloguing in Publication Data**
The North Pennines landscape: a landscape assessment prepared
by Land Use Consultants for the Countryside Commission.
1. England (Mountains)
I. Great Britain. *Countryside Commission 914.28*
ISBN 0-86170-279-4

Cover: *Farms in Upper Teesdale from the Alston road.* (Simon Warner)

Designed and produced by Imaging – Cheltenham
Printed by Cotswold Printing Company – Stroud

*The North Pennines – an outstanding landscape.*

# Foreword

The North Pennines is the largest area of outstanding natural beauty (AONB) in England and Wales. It lies between the Northumberland and Yorkshire Dales National Parks. Its beauty was identified by Dower and Hobhouse in the 1940s, but it was not until 1988 that its designation as an AONB was confirmed, following an exhaustive public inquiry which centred on the landscape beauty of the area.

Few who know the area would doubt its special beauty but, in commissioning this study by Land Use Consultants, we aim to define more clearly the character and value of this AONB. Such assessments will now be conducted for all AONBs as a means of better understanding their particular quality and character, and thus taking more informed decisions on planning and land management issues. This book is the fifth of a series: previous publications have examined the New Forest, the Blackdown Hills, the Cotswolds and the Cambrian Mountains.

Our purpose in publishing the report is to set down in some detail the special qualities of this little-known area. The report outlines how the landscape was formed and how it is managed. It details the variety to be found within the AONB, from the high moorland to each of the intimate dales, and examines how the natural beauty of the area has been perceived through time. Finally, it draws attention to the current forces for change.

We hope that this book will not only provide food for thought for the professional wrestling with land management issues in this beautiful area, but that it will also raise awareness and understanding amongst those who may wish to visit this remote part of England.

DEREK BARBER
Chairman
Countryside Commission

# Preface

The aim of this study was to conduct a landscape survey of the North Pennines AONB, and to prepare a report that describes the landscape and its various components, defines its special landscape character and quality, identifies the current influences on the landscape and their likely consequences, and describes the role of forestry and woodlands in the character of the area.

In carrying out this work, we have been guided by the contents of the Countryside Commission guidelines on landscape assessment (1), and by our own particular experience in upland areas. The method used in this work is similar to that described in another report in this series, *The Cambrian Mountains landscape* (2). In essence, it has involved desk study of relevant background material, map analysis and preparation of overlays showing geology, topography and land cover, field survey, research into perception of the landscape, judgements about its importance, and assessment of current forces for change.

We have set out the conclusions drawn from these studies, concentrating upon the following issues:

- the forces involved in shaping the landscape, both historically and at present;

- the special features that are typical of the North Pennines landscape;

- the division of the area into a number of recognisable landscape types, and description of the particular characteristics of each type;

- information about the way in which the landscape has been perceived and appreciated over the years;

- a summary of the special character and quality of the area that makes it of national importance.

Land Use Consultants
January 1991

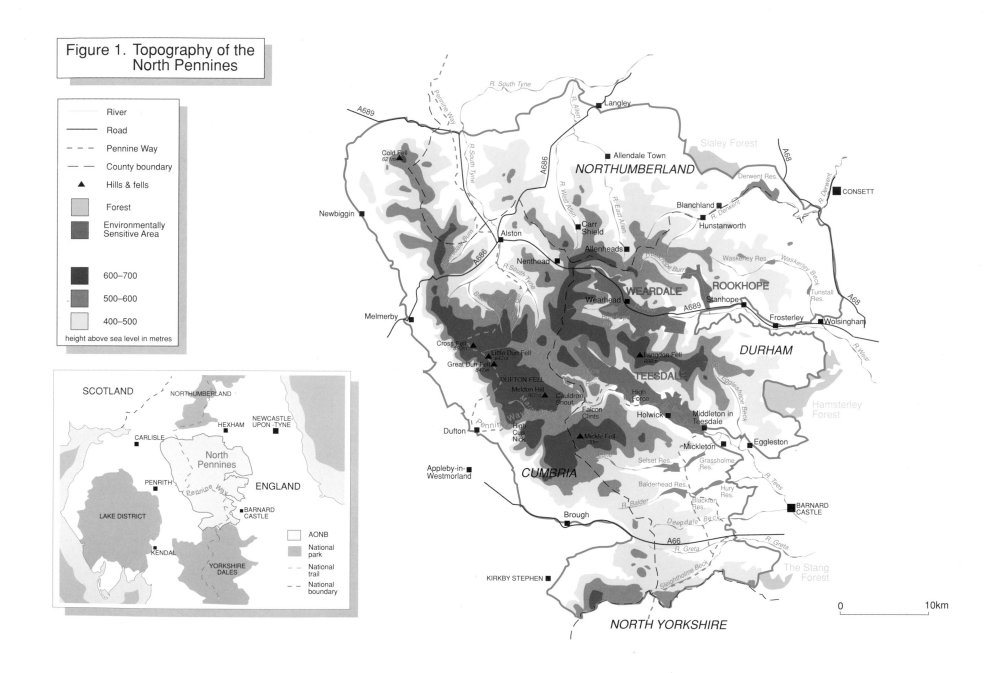

Figure 1. Topography of the North Pennines

**Legend:**
- River
- Road
- Pennine Way
- County boundary
- ▲ Hills & fells
- Forest
- Environmentally Sensitive Area
- 600–700
- 500–600
- 400–500

height above sea level in metres

**Inset map legend:**
- AONB
- National park
- National trail
- National boundary

# 1. Introduction to the North Pennines landscape

The wild moorlands of the North Pennines have seen many battles and skirmishes over the centuries, from the battles of Viking kings, to cross-border raids by bands of reivers from Scotland, to the infamous 'battle of the Bonny-Moor-Hen', a skirmish between miners and gamekeepers over rights to the red grouse. More recently, in 1985, the area was the subject of a unique modern skirmish which, in a prolonged battle of words, examined in great detail the beauty of the landscape.

This bloodless skirmish was a public inquiry to investigate whether the North Pennines should be designated as an area of outstanding natural beauty (AONB). It was the first ever public examination of such a proposal, and as such gave a fascinating insight into the wide range of views that are held about the character and qualities of this wild, upland area. After all the deliberations, decisions were taken and the area was duly confirmed as an AONB in 1988. The purpose of this report is to set down clearly what it is that makes the North Pennines landscape so important and so worthy of special protection.

The North Pennines lie, as their name suggests, at the northern end of the Pennine chain of uplands. They are a distinct and separate block of upland moorland and dales, lying immediately adjacent to the Yorkshire Dales National Park to the south, separated from Northumberland National Park to the north by the Tyne Gap, and from the Lake District to the west by the Vale of Eden (see Figure 1). The whole region is thus rich in diverse and attractive landscapes, and the North Pennines are no exception to this. They embrace two broadly contrasting types of landscape, combining some of the highest, wildest moorland summits in England, with the more domestic, agricultural scenery of the dales that divide the upland masses.

Most of the area is bleak and remote, and levels of population are low. The North Pennines include some of the highest settlements in England, such as Alston, Allenheads and Nenthead, and the upland conditions are harsh. Only three major roads pass through the North Pennines: the A686 from Penrith to Haydon Bridge cuts across the western scarp and through the moorland summits; the A689 passes from Brampton, south through South Tynedale and Weardale; the infamous A66 trans-Pennine route from Scotch Corner to Penrith cuts across the Stainmore Gap on the same line as prehistoric and Roman routes.

The landscape of the North Pennines as we see it today has been shaped by both the physical influences of geology and climate, and the human influences of settlement and land use history.

## Physical influences on the landscape

Geologically, the North Pennines are formed by what is known as the Alston Block, which is bounded to the north and west by great faults. The Tyne Gap fault divides the North Pennines from the Northumberland Moors to the north, and the fault to the west is dramatically manifested by a steep scarp running the length of the western boundary of the AONB, where the older rocks of the North Pennine moors rise above the New Red Sandstone of the Vale of Eden. The Alston Block is gently tilted to the east and eventually dips below the Durham coalfields.

The area is dominated by rocks of the Carboniferous period, forming sequential layers of thin coal, sandstone, shale and limestone – known as the Yoredale series (see Figure 2). These rhythmic layers are a result of past marine invasions, deltaic and swamp conditions. They give many of the dale sides their characteristic stepped appearance, because of differential resistance to weathering of each layer. In the west, the uplifting of the Alston Block has resulted in the erosion of the upper layers of the Yoredale series to reveal the underlying limestone and lower Palaeozoic shales. However, to the east, as the Block dips away, the more recent Carboniferous formations of Millstone Grit and Coal Measures remain, and are the predominant influence on the landscape.

During the late Carboniferous period, volcanic activity caused igneous intrusions into the Yoredale series, forming thick, quartz-dolerite sheets between the layers. The subsequent movement of the Carboniferous strata, by faulting and folding, resulted in the exposure, to dramatic scenic effect, of these resistant igneous 'sheets', known as the Whin Sill. This effect is demonstrated by well known features such as High Cup, Cauldron Snout, High Force and Cronkley Scar. The heat associated with these igneous intrusions also caused localised metamorphosis of the surrounding rocks, forming unusual, coarse-crystalled 'sugar limestone' from limestone, and whetstone from sandstone.

The welling up of molten material from below caused the Alston Block to dome upwards and created many minor faults. These faults, including vertical fractures and some widened bedding planes, filled with super-heated, mineral-bearing solution from the granite below, which then cooled to form deposits of silver-rich galena (lead ore), barytes, pyrite and ankerite (iron ores), zinc ore, witherite, calcite, fluorspar, and quartz. These deposits, called ore shoots, varied from several inches to several feet in thickness and were generally richest in the Great Limestone strata. Where they occurred on or near the surface, many of these minerals have subsequently been worked, giving rise to the mining industry that has had such an influence on the landscape.

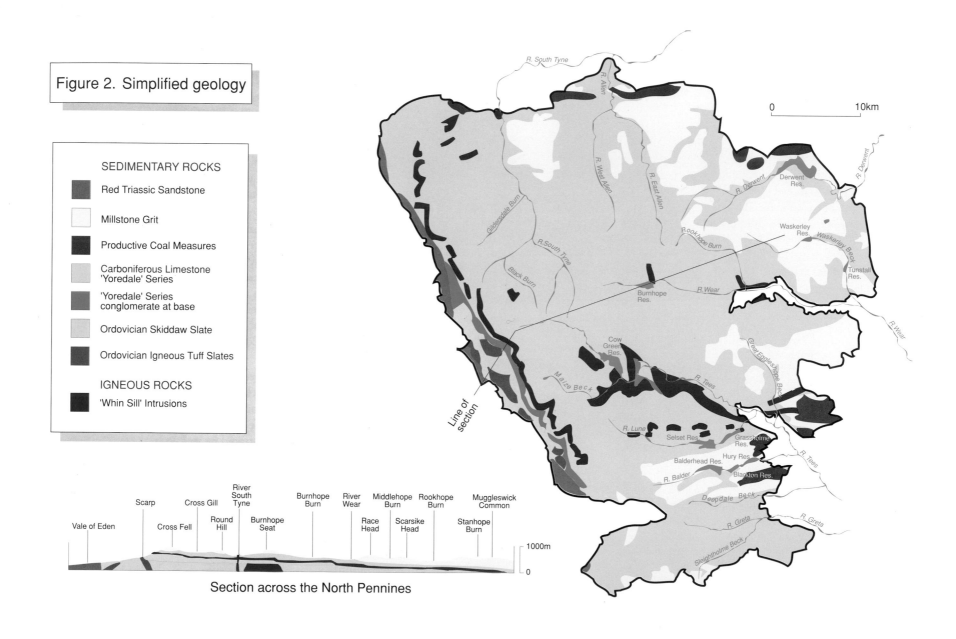

## Figure 2. Simplified geology

**SEDIMENTARY ROCKS**

- Red Triassic Sandstone
- Millstone Grit
- Productive Coal Measures
- Carboniferous Limestone 'Yoredale' Series
- 'Yoredale' Series conglomerate at base
- Ordovician Skiddaw Slate
- Ordovician Igneous Tuff Slates

**IGNEOUS ROCKS**

- 'Whin Sill' Intrusions

0        10km

Line of section

R. South Tyne
R. Allen
R. West Allen
R. East Allen
R. Derwent
Derwent Res.
R. Derwent
Gilderstdale Burn
R. South Tyne
Rookhope Burn
Waskerley Res.
Waskerley Beck
Tunstall Res.
Black Burn
Burnhope Res.
R. Wear
R. Wear
Cow Green Res.
Maize Beck
R. Tees
Great Eggleshope Beck
R. Lune
Selset Res.
Grassholme Res.
Hury Res.
Balderhead Res.
Blackton Res.
R. Balder
R. Tees
Deepdale Beck
R. Greta
R. Greta
Sleightholme Beck

Vale of Eden
Scarp
Cross Fell
Cross Gill
Round Hill
River South Tyne
Burnhope Seat
Burnhope Burn
River Wear
Race Head
Middlehope Burn
Scarsike Head
Rookhope Burn
Stanhope Burn
Muggleswick Common

1000m
0

### Section across the North Pennines

The high moorland summits, which run the length of the western edge of the area above the scarp bounding the Vale of Eden, are the source of all of the major drainage channels of the North Pennines (see Figure 3). Cross Fell in particular, the highest point along this undulating ridge, is the centre for the drainage pattern which fans out to the north and east. These moorland gathering grounds, fed by high levels of rainfall, are drained by six main rivers and their associated tributaries. To the east, the River Wear and the River Tees follow the tilt of the Alston Block and cut long, broad dales. To the north, shorter dales are formed by the rivers South Tyne, East and West Allen, Derwent and Devil's Water, all joining the Tyne that flows from west to east through the Tyne Gap to the north. These north-flowing rivers display an asymmetric valley cross-section, due to the later uplift of the Alston Block that is thought to have caused the rivers to undercut their eastern banks.

The effect of glaciation in modifying the relief of the North Pennines is mainly manifested by deposition rather than by the erosive action of ice, although the main dales do show some evidence of widening and deepening by ice action. From the escarpment above the Vale of Eden, the effect of the deposition of boulder clay can be clearly seen as drumlins on the valley floor. Similar features are also present in Teesdale and Weardale. The other major impact of glaciation on the area has been the effect of meltwater cutting many channels, particularly in the scarp face itself. This also provided the erosive power to create many of the characteristic features of the limestone areas, such as cave systems and natural bridges. Other typical limestone features, including pavements and crags, occur where the rock is exposed and weathered.

The persistence of periglacial (ie, freezing but not full-scale glacial) conditions since the last ice age, around Cross Fell and the Upper Tees, has given rise to other rare features such as stone stripes, circles and polygons, solifluction terraces and hummocks formed by frost heave. Associated with these unusual physiological features and the climatic conditions is a flora that is unique in England.

The drift deposits of the North Pennines falls into three types, namely: boulder clay, which is mainly confined to the Vale of Eden and the dales; peat, formed since the last ice age, which covers the high moorland summits; and glacial sands and gravel, alluvium and river terrace deposits which are found in some of the river corridors and flood plains.

## Human influences on the landscape

Man's first colonisation of, and therefore impact on, the North Pennines goes back to perhaps 7,000 BC, when nomadic mesolithic hunters are thought to have had temporary campsites in the area. Woodland was at its most extensive at this time and covered the whole area, apart perhaps from the highest peaks above 750 metres. It is thought that the hunters may have started the reduction of the woodland area. Clearance intensified after 3,000 BC with the activities of Neolithic farmers–hunters.

*There are visible reminders of many eras of human influence on the landscape, such as this Roman fortification at Whitley Castle.*

### Settlement history

The subsequent settlement history is one of continued forest clearance and the formation and expansion of peat. The existence of prehistoric farming and settlement is demonstrated by the presence of burial mounds such as the one at Kirkhaugh in the South Tyne Valley. It is likely that farming was concentrated in the same areas as it is today. The remains of these early farms are, therefore, buried beneath later landscapes; nevertheless, aerial photography has recently begun to demonstrate the extent of early settlement. There have been discoveries of Bronze-Age field systems in Stainmore, Teesdale and Weardale, where Bronze-Age field boundaries can be found at heights of over 450 metres on what is now open moorland.

In the Roman period, the area formed part of the military/frontier zone and was crossed by a number of roads. Early exploitation of lead deposits is shown by the presence of ingots at Brough, and perhaps by the siting and strong defences of Whitley Castle. That the area still contained much woodland is shown by pollen evidence, the dedication of an altar to Silvanus, and by later records containing complaints about the felling and destruction of woodlands at that time.

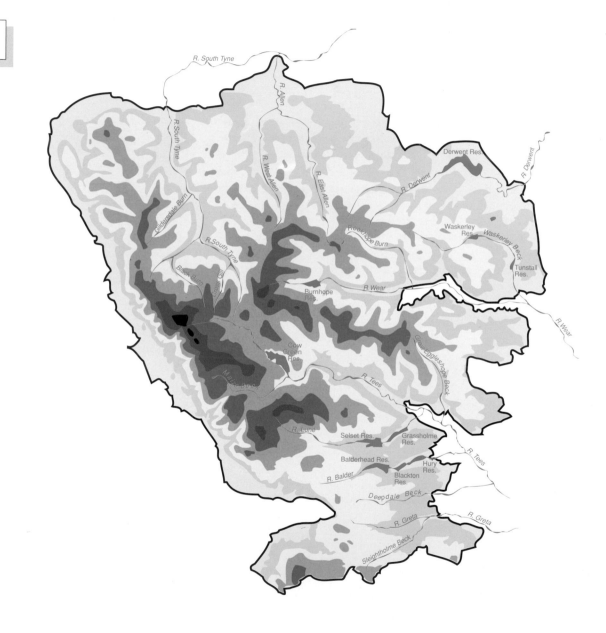

Figure 3.  Physical features

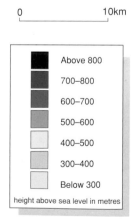

Above 800
700–800
600–700
500–600
400–500
300–400
Below 300

height above sea level in metres

0          10km

While we know little of farming methods in the Roman and Prehistoric periods, it is probable that there was a system of cattle rearing and limited cereal cultivation. It is also likely that transhumance was widely practised – having developed from the need, in a largely forested landscape, to exploit natural grassland away from the main settlement. This pattern of land use and settlement continued in the medieval period, and may also have been linked in later times with seasonal mining of, for example, coal. Certainly, the need to move cattle and sheep between the common grazing lands and settlements led to the incorporation of lanes and droveways through the enclosed lands.

By 100 BC the whole of the Pennines was controlled by a single tribal group, the Brigantes. From the sixth century, the Anglian Kingdom of Northumbria was established after invasion by the Angles and other Germanic invaders. The spread of Anglian settlements can be determined by analysis of place names. Names ending in -ley, -ing, -ham or -ton are of Anglian origin. Villages ending in -ley were the original settlements, created by small communities clearing woodland in the lower dales, usually in Millstone Grit country with heavy woodland, where the soils were suitable for arable and pastoral farming. Villages ending with -ing or -ham were originally homesteads, often pioneering settlements higher up the dales in limestone country. Those ending in -ton were originally farmsteads, often satellites to larger settlements, concentrating on pastoral farming and generally found further west in limestone country. Examples of the main Anglian settlements in and around the North Pennines are Middleton and Eggleston in Teesdale, and Wolsingham and Frosterley in Weardale.

By the late ninth century, the Danes had conquered Northumbria, and Danish settlements were being developed between the existing Anglian villages. The Danes moved through the Stainmore Gap and down the Vale of Eden, establishing many new settlements there. Danish place names generally ended in -by and -thorp. The main settlements were -by villages occupying similar country to the Anglian -ley villages (and sometimes renaming them), or satellite settlements near to existing Anglian villages or larger -by villages. Examples in the area are the scarp-foot villages of Melmerby and Gamblesby in the Vale of Eden.

In the tenth century the Norse appeared. This was the time of Eric Bloodaxe. The Norse settled the fell lands and valley-head areas and practised pastoral farming, concentrating on sheep rearing. These upland areas were generally neglected and only sparsely settled by the existing population. The Norse were therefore able to settle without greatly disturbing the existing communities. Indeed, Norse settlements were rather isolated. Transhumance continued to be practised, making best use of the moorland areas. Few sizeable Norse settlements were established, but many of the names given to the features of the upland landscape remain as evidence of their influence: scale, sett, thwaite, fell, gill, slack and moss are all words of Norse origin. The Norse Kingdom ended with the death of Eric Bloodaxe in 954 at Stainmore.

The next major influence on the settlement of the North Pennines was the establishment by the Norman invaders of large 'honours'. These were feudally controlled areas, based perhaps on earlier existing estates. These were the Palatine Bishopric of Durham, the Honour of Richmond (south of the Tees), the Bishopric of Wilfred (Allendale, Mid Tynedale, Devil's Water and north-west Hexhamshire) and Aldenstane Moor (later Alston Moor). The Bishopric of Durham, established early in the eleventh century, had perhaps the greatest influence on the development of the area. A great hunting forest, centred on Weardale, was established, and two new villages were developed at the east and west gate of the forest (now Eastgate and Westgate). The feudal economy forced changes in agriculture, and specialist skills and industries flourished in the service of the church and Norman overlords.

The church, and particularly monastic orders, were responsible for significant developments in the north of England. In Yorkshire, the Cistercians built some of the finest monasteries in the country during the twelfth century. In the North Pennines, the less well-known Premonstratensian order built monasteries at Blanchland in Derwentdale and at Egglestone in Teesdale. The former was destroyed and the present village built around the remains.

## The mining industry

Lead was first discovered in the area during Roman times, but the more significant discoveries and early workings were on Alston Moor (then Aldenstane) in the twelfth century. Other minerals were also worked, and a Royal Mint was established at Carlisle to make coins from silver, mined at what were known as 'the silver mines of Carlisle' on Alston Moor. Metalliferous mining has taken place in the area since these early workings, and especially in the period from the fourteenth to the nineteenth centuries. This has had a major effect on the landscape. The ore shoots in the limestone have been a rich and accessible source of minerals and have been exploited for hundreds of years. Early mining was concerned primarily with the lead, silver and iron ores, but latterly the commercial value of other minerals, used more widely in modern industry, encouraged mining companies to extend their range, and to rework old mining sites for minerals previously thought to be of little value.

Before the expansion of the industry, the hills and dales of the North Pennines were sparsely populated, with the older settlements and most densely populated areas situated in the sheltered lower dales. Metalliferous and, in particular, lead mining, and the industry it generated and supported, caused the rapid expansion of existing settlements in the mining areas. Alston became the centre of the industry. Lead was then discovered in Weardale, and mines were developed by the Bishop of Durham

*Remains of the lead mining industry are widespread. The arch (above) in the valley of Rookhope is a good example, as are old spoil heaps (below), now re-vegetated, in the same area.*

*Striking reminders of the industrial past can be found high on the moorland landscape.*

after leases were granted by the King. By the fourteenth century, people were starting to move into the mining areas. This influx, and the opening of new mining areas, led to the establishment of a series of new villages and remote mining communities, and to the settlement of substantial areas in the upper dales. In the seventeenth century, the industry grew enormously, and during the eighteenth and nineteenth centuries the North Pennines developed into one of the most productive mining areas in Britain and Europe.

Lead mining activity has been extensive, although the scale of operation has varied over the centuries. There were particular concentrations of mining activity in Upper Weardale between Killhope and Nenthead, in Weardale north west of Stanhope, around Nenthead, at Allenheads, in West Allendale around Carr Shield, in the valley of the Rookhope Burn, to the north of Teesdale and in Derwentdale near Ramshaw. Communities grew up near these centres of mining activity, with some villages being purpose-built by the mining companies, such as at Allenheads (Blackett – Beaumont Mining Company) and at Nenthead (London Lead Company). The mining regions rapidly became some of the most intensively developed upland areas in Britain. By the mid- to late-nineteenth century, through a combination of inward migration and high birth rates, population figures in the North Pennines reached their peak, with a population in 1861 of some 27,000 in the ore field areas (Alston, Allendale, Stanhope and parts of Derwent and Teesdale). Development in the dales to accommodate this growth spread initially along the valley floor, first with the expansion of existing settlements, then with the development of new villages. These villages were sometimes built in such close proximity to each other that building development was almost continuous, as, for example, at St. John's Chapel, Cowshill, Daddry Shield and Ireshopeburn in Weardale.

The London Lead Company gave their employees small-holdings, to ensure healthy outdoor activity to counteract the effects of mine work, and to ensure that food would not need to be imported. Mining and farming thus became interdependent, and continued to be so over the years.

The miner–farmers established small-holdings and cultivated land at unusually high altitudes. As well as livestock, diverse small-scale vegetable and cereal growing was practised, and in extensive areas there developed a patchwork of small, geometric enclosures with their stone walls and attendant cottages or farmsteads. These upland enclosures were cultivated and improved by use of lime applications. Limestone was quarried locally and burnt in limekilns to produce 'quick lime' for fertiliser and for building construction. Limekilns of various sizes became common features, and many ruined limekilns remain today. Pastoral farming formerly extended up to a height of some 300 metres, with rough moorland grazing above this. However, the mining small-holdings were responsible for extending this limit to more inhospitable areas, up to a height of 550 metres, especially in the dale heads. Arguably, the effects on the landscape of this dual economy and its related settlement pattern were as significant as those of the mining activity itself.

An important feature of the lead industry was that it was not only extractive, but a complete process involving mining, dressing and smelting. It generated a wide range of ancillary industries which extended the influence of the mining industry throughout the North Pennines area. The expansion of settlements, and the construction of roads, rail and tramways, reservoirs and water supply lines within and outside the main mining areas, are examples of some of the related developments that affected the landscape.

The decline of the mining industry, beginning in the late nineteenth century, caused major changes both to communities and to the landscape. The mines were abandoned and they, and the many associated structures and features, fell into decay. Some were gradually absorbed back into the landscape, but there are still a great many visible remains today, which provide an important record of an industry that was vital to the area for centuries. Many small-holdings were abandoned and have been absorbed into larger farms or estates. Buildings have become redundant and ruined. The high field enclosures are seldom cultivated and have reverted to marginal grazing and moorland. Nevertheless, the legacy of field patterns and isolated buildings in a remote upland landscape is an important characteristic of the North Pennines. Together with the extensive remains of mining activity itself, it tells the story of an era of history and a way of life that thrived as a result of the natural resources of the landscape.

Although the lead mining industry declined so dramatically, other forms of mining and quarrying have continued in the area and in adjacent settlements. While sometimes causing damage to the landscape, these activities have helped to maintain the population and support the communities in the area, ensuring that the landscape remains a living landscape. Quarrying of limestone, sandstone, ganister and Whin Sill outcrops, mining of fluorspar and barytes, and small-scale coal mining, have all influenced the landscape and continue, to a varying extent, to do so.

## Hill and upland farming

There is relatively little remaining evidence of the activities of the earliest prehistoric farmers in the North Pennines, although new archaeological evidence is coming to light which suggests that much of the area was cleared and being farmed by 1500 BC. Some lynchets, or terraces, remaining on the dale sides provide evidence of prehistoric and Roman farming, as well as of later periods. The Anglian settlers established farms and fields in the dales and carried out further forest clearance for pasture and fell grazing. Anglian villages had common fields for arable farming and common pastures and meadows in the dales. Many of the early farmers, from prehistoric times onwards, practised transhumance, and seasonal shelters or 'shielings' were built at high levels.

When the Norman deer forests were established, many of the Norse settlement areas were absorbed into them and sheep grazing was restricted. There were certainly forests and deer in both Weardale and Teesdale. At the end of the twelfth century, it is probable that the dales consisted of a pattern of arable and pasture land, set in woodland, that spread up the dale sides to open, grazed moorland above. In the dale heads there were probably scattered Norse farmsteads amidst continuous forest.

With the first workings of lead, the population began to grow, and the lords of the manor allowed more clearing and settlement in the deer forests in exchange for rent or services. As the control of the feudal estates diminished, more of the land was divided up amongst smaller owner-occupiers. In the thirteenth century, colonisation had pushed settlement up to heights of more than 450 metres. By the sixteenth century, the pressure for farmland had increased, so open fields around the villages were subdivided, and new intakes of pasture were created further up the hill. Common grazing on the fells played a very important role, and grazing was often 'stinted' by allocating farmers rights to graze fixed numbers of stock. Despite the many castles built for protection, raids from Scotland, which had been common over the centuries, continued to make farming risky until the Act of Union with Scotland.

Fragmentation of land holdings intensified during the sixteenth, seventeenth and eighteenth centuries as pressure for land increased, fuelled by the boom in lead mining and the desire of farmers and landowners to improve their land and rents. The enclosure acts in the period from 1770 to 1820 authorised the subdivision of meadows and pastures into smaller units, and the enclosure of larger areas of previously stinted common fell-grazing to form intermediate pastures or allotments, which divided the valley pastures and meadows from the commons and moorland tops. Local stone was used to build the characteristic field walls and new farmsteads and farm buildings that are an important characteristic of the landscape today.

Despite the enclosure acts of the eighteenth and nineteenth centuries, substantial areas of common land still remain as remnants of the manorial system of the Middle Ages, embracing substantial tracts of high moorland. These commons, as well as some of the enclosed moors, are often dominated by heather that supports large populations of red grouse. Grouse have been a highly-prized resource for many years, as evidenced by the 1818 'battle' between miners and gamekeepers in Weardale. The North Pennine moors are reputed to be among the best in the world for grouse and attract guns from far afield. Such sport has its own effect on the landscape, especially through the burning of heather that is essential to maintain the right conditions for the grouse. This produces a marked and characteristic mosaic pattern, of burnt patches and strips and heather of different ages.

Large estates, such as the Raby and Strathmore estates, have had a significant role in maintaining the landscape over the years, by influencing the use and management of very large areas of farmland, woodland and moorland. Their influence can be clearly seen in the characteristic white-painted farm buildings of the Raby estate, a notable feature of the landscape in Teesdale.

Upland farming has continued to be the main land use, with the emphasis on rearing of sheep and cattle. Most of the income comes from sheep flocks, which are grazed on common land, on other moorland grazing, and on allotment land and in-bye pastures. Upland farms, as opposed to hill farms, tend to have more enclosed pastures and gain income more equally from cattle and sheep. Over the years, this type of farming has continued to maintain the traditional landscape, and change has been relatively limited. Increases in stocking levels have led to changes in the moorland vegetation, with high sheep numbers encouraging varieties of grass to replace heather and other shrub vegetation. Some moorland has been reclaimed, generally at the margins of viable cultivation, and some meadows and pastures in the dales have been improved by drainage, fertilising and re-seeding, although many remain as unimproved flower-rich hay meadows.

Agricultural land has been lost to other activities, notably water storage and supply. This has led to the introduction of a number of new reservoirs in the area. These include, amongst others, reservoirs in Lunedale (Grassholme and Selset Reservoirs), in Baldersdale (Balderhead, Blackton and Hury Reservoirs) off Weardale (Tunstall Reservoir), in Derwentdale (Derwent Reservoir) and in Upper Teesdale (Cow Green Reservoir), added to the significant number of small reservoirs left by the mining industry. The larger reservoirs have inundated significant areas of in-bye pasture and meadow, as well as, in the case of Cow Green, rare upland flora. Commercial forestry has also appeared, although the larger areas such as Hamsterly Forest and Slaley Forest lie just outside the AONB, and the scale of planting in the area has not been large.

Today, the landscape is the combined result of all of these influences, both physical and historical, and it is changed from day to day by the ephemeral effects of changes in weather, in light conditions, and by seasonal effects of colour and texture. The result is that, while the North Pennines is undoubtedly a single landscape unit, there are complex and subtle variations that create a wide range of different landscape types, as well as a number of special features of interest that occur throughout the AONB.

# 2. Features of the landscape

There are certain features that make a particular contribution to the North Pennines landscape and help to give it its special value. They are described briefly below.

## Geological and landform features

The North Pennines AONB contains a large number of unique and spectacular geological and landform features. The most impressive of these are also among the most familiar. Some have a long history as visitor attractions, and most are on the route of the Pennine Way.

The Whin Sill creates some of the most striking features. It is a blue-black, crystalline rock known as quartz dolerite, which is very hard and resistant to weathering, and forms either marked vertical columns in cliffs, or strange, shiny steps and blocks when worn away by rivers. This rock stands out from the surrounding scenery in many places because of its relatively greater resistance to erosion. The

*Geological and landform features, such as the dramatic U-shaped valley of High Cup, are a striking characteristic of the landscape.*

River Tees illustrates this spectacularly along its course, as it cascades over the Whin Sill in waterfalls, first at Cauldron Snout then at High Force and finally Low Force, and winds between the spectacular outcropping crags of Falcon Clints, Cronkley Scar, Holwick Scar and Crossthwaite Scar. These features combine to make this stretch of the Tees a rugged blend of beauty and power. Travelling westwards from Teesdale over the high moors along the Pennine Way, the Whin Sill is encountered again, at one of the most inspiring views along its length. Approaching the top of the scarp that forms the western limit of the AONB, the ground suddenly swoops away in graceful curves in the spectacular feature of High Cup, a perfectly symmetrical U-shaped valley, carved into the scarp face and edged by dark vertical cliffs of Whin Sill rock with a silver ribbon of water far below.

Other landform features are perhaps less spectacular, although equally important in the landscape. The influence of the underlying limestone geology creates a wide range of interesting features, although they are not of the same scale and extent as the limestone scenery of the Craven area of the Yorkshire Dales. Limestone is exposed and has been weathered to pavements in a number of locations, notably in the south west of the AONB near Brough. Other features associated with 'karst scenery' are also present. Often the most visible evidence is in the form of numerous 'shake holes'. These are depressions through which water may enter and pass along an underground course. In a number of places these courses have been enlarged by the rock above collapsing, creating gorges, caves and natural bridges. These features, although less numerous than in the Yorkshire Dales, can be very dramatic, and include Sleightholme Beck gorge and God's Bridge near the Pennine Way in the south of the area, and the less visible but equally important caves such as Knock Fell cave and Fairy Holes cave in Weardale.

The complex layers of the Yoredale series of rocks create several important features. These include the stepped appearance of many of the dale sides, clearly visible, for example, in South Tynedale, and the well-known series of flat-topped moorland summits which are the highest points in the area. The high summits, including Cross Fell, Great Dun Fell, Mickle Fell and Knock Fell are formed of harder-wearing caps of coarse sandstone, and stand proud of the surrounding moorland, each with its own distinctive profile.

The summits have their own particular character, being generally flat and grassy but punctuated by stone cairns in places. Cross Fell is particularly important for the features formed by the seasonal freezing and thawing of the ground, notably stone stripes and polygons. Such features are normally found in the Lake District and in Scotland.

## Flora and fauna

The particular geology, climate and land use history of the North Pennines combine to produce a range of habitats and a flora and fauna of outstanding interest and value. A wide range of habitats occurs, including: extensive areas of blanket bog, with heather and cotton grass dominant; other acid moorland habitats, including valley bog, dry heath, acid grassland and bracken; limestone grasslands including unusual and rare types found on the 'sugar' limestone of Upper Teesdale; neutral grasslands on the richer valley soils, notably the unimproved species rich hay meadows; and a range of native woodlands.

One of the most important habitats is limestone grassland, which contains a very high number of different types of plants including an unusual number of rare species. The sugar limestone grasslands of Upper Teesdale are particularly important because they include arctic-alpine or alpine flora and a great number of very unusual species. It is said that no other limestone grassland in Britain is so rich in rare plant species. The value of this area is further increased by the presence of juniper scrub, which is scarce and on the decline in Britain.

*The North Pennines is uniquely important for nature conservation, with a range of special habitats including extensive heather moorland.*

The hay meadows, especially those of the upper dales, are also valued because they are rich in plant species and include a large number of rare and local species. It is thought that these hay meadows may be the remains of the flora of woodlands that grew on the same sites many centuries ago, because they include some plants typical of woodland, such as globe flowers and wood anemones. Traditional management over the centuries, without drainage, addition of fertiliser other than lime or manure, or other forms of improvement, has created and maintained the rich grasslands.

The moorland areas are important primarily because of the extent of uninterrupted blanket bog. At Moorhouse, the moorland forms an internationally important 'Biosphere Reserve'. There are also unusual types of habitat, including limestone heath, formed where acid soils occur over limestone, where acid-loving plants grow alongside limestone species. Such an extent of moorland habitat supports a typical and diverse bird population. Commoner species such as grouse, curlew, lapwing and skylark are an integral and familiar part of the sights and sounds of the moorland landscape. Other birds are less easily seen because of their comparative rarity, but the area has breeding populations of a number of protected bird species. Merlin, peregrine, golden plover, snipe, redshank, dotterel, dunlin and blackcock are all important birds of the upland moors.

The range of flora and fauna gives the area unique nature conservation importance. Equally, this range of habitats and species is an inseparable part of the special landscape character of the area. The patterns of moorland vegetation, the flowering of the heather, the bright flower-strewn meadows in spring and early summer, the sounds of the moorland birds which strike the ear as soon as one passes from dale to moor, are all a major part of what makes the North Pennines special.

## Buildings and settlements

The buildings and settlements of the North Pennines are an integral part of the landscape. Most are built of local stone, reflecting the underlying geology, complementing the stone field walls, and generally making a significant contribution to the unity of the landscape.

Although many of the settlements have early origins, little remains of the earliest buildings. Anglian, Danish and Norse buildings were usually built of timber and wattle and were easily destroyed. Before the fifteenth century, only a few buildings were constructed entirely of stone. They included castles, pele towers, monasteries, priories, churches and large houses. Some of these remain intact, although perhaps modified, but several stand as impressive ruins. The castles built to counter the raids by the Scots are perhaps the most significant structures of this type. Most remaining examples lie outside the area, although Staward Pele in lower Allendale, built on a high crag over the Allen gorges, is a good example. Some existing farmhouses also began as Tudor castles.

*Buildings in the landscape include many simple small-holdings, often marked by a tree clump.*

*Larger farmsteads are often vernacular stone buildings on a 'long house' pattern.*

*Many small villages, such as Garrigill in South Tynedale, add to the character of the landscape.*

*Alston is an attractive market town much influenced by its mining history.*

Church building started in the late seventh century, although few of these early examples were permanent structures. In the medieval period, ecclesiastical building was vigorous in Yorkshire, but relatively few structures were built in the North Pennines. The most notable examples, just outside the AONB, are Wolsingham Church, Stanhope Church and Eggleston Monastery and, within the AONB, the monastery at Blanchland, now incorporated into the village. A small number of true vernacular buildings remain from the fourteenth century, when stone became more widely used amongst the yeoman class. At the same time, stone masons who had worked on castles and abbeys became available to work on manor houses and the 'granges' of monasteries. This led to two types of medieval development – large houses often designed in the Tudor style, and vernacular houses and cottages built as stone replicas of their timber and wattle predecessors.

The houses of the richer yeoman class are far fewer north of the Stainmore Gap than south of it in the Yorkshire Dales, because of the hardship and less profitable nature of agriculture and the mining industry. The vernacular style of houses and cottages predominates in the North Pennines. Although most of the buildings in the landscape date from the seventeenth century or later, they varied little from generation to generation.

The earliest common type of building structure that used timber and stone was the 'crucked' building. This used curved tree trunks, 'cruck blades', as the main roof supports, and had horizontal ties and purlins between the ridge and eaves levels to provide stability. Stone was used to fill below the eaves and for the gables. The 'cruck' system formed bays along the building. It was easy to extend the length of a crucked building, but difficult to make additions onto the side, unless they were small lean-to structures below eaves level. The dimensions and horizontal nature of the early 'crucked' structures determined to a large extent the architectural form and proportions of later 'vernacular' building types in the North Pennines. They were constructed between the thirteenth and sixteenth centuries, although very few remain in their original form. The cruck structures were replaced by more conventional roof trusses, the stone wall increased in height, and the angle of the roof was reduced to approximately 30°.

Evolution from these early crucked structures established the typical characteristics of the majority of North Pennine buildings. They are basic, rubble stone buildings of gritstone or sometimes limestone, of horizontal form and usually with two storeys. The roofs have shallow pitch and are covered with gritstone slabs, or Lake District slates in the western areas. The slabs are generally coursed and become smaller near the ridge. The windows are square with plain lintels and sill or, rarely, mullion. . The larger buildings are of 'long house' plan, often with a porch extension that is covered by an extension of the roof at the same angle. Variations on the basic building type occur in small houses, cottages and large houses, and also in stone field barns.

Farmsteads are an important part of the landscape. Some are built in defensive squares, occasionally with pele towers. However, the majority are cottages and small houses built by the miner-farmers. They have barns attached in the traditional long-house plan, either under the same, or a lower roof. They were usually built along the contours, facing up and down the hill, and are often accompanied by a clump of trees.

Sometimes they are whitewashed, particularly in Teesdale, to identify property on the Raby estate. Free-standing field barns or hog-houses scattered throughout the dales are of similar form, but are only a single bay long.

In the villages and towns there is a more complex mixture of building types, with replacement and infill adding new styles. There are three basic types of village. The scarp-foot villages were built in red sandstone with slate or sandstone roofs. A number have a defensive layout around a village green, and are clearly planned settlements. Older Anglian villages have a long history and a mix of different types of building. Most, such as Middleton-in-Teesdale, Eggleston, Wolsingham and Frosterley, lie on the fringes of the area. Industrial mining settlements were developed as a result of the expanding mining industry, and were often purpose-built by the mining companies. Some were new, but others were added on to existing settlements. They include Allenheads, Nenthead and the string of settlements in the middle and upper part of Weardale.

Churches are notable buildings in all of the villages, particularly the Methodist chapels, which are often almost vernacular in style. Other public buildings, such as schools and libraries, generally result from the efforts of the mining companies to serve their communities. They demonstrate departures from the vernacular style that took place in the eighteenth century. Industrialisation provided finance for 'polite' architecture, and Georgian influences introduced more classical dimensions, more cubic proportions and more verticality, plus porticoes, symmetrical facades, sash windows, dressed stone and slate roofs.

Other exceptional villages that do not fall into one of these three broad types are Blanchland and Hunstanworth, in Derwentdale. Blanchland is now a remarkably picturesque and popular estate village, built in the nineteenth century on and around the remains of an old monastery. Hunstanworth, nearby, also demonstrates in its few buildings, a planned layout and coordinated design, with notable geometrically patterned roof tiles.

## The agricultural landscape

The dales are of archaeological importance, because of the evidence that remains of old field systems, dating back to the earliest settlements. Strip lynchets still occur in places, and are easily visible in the right light conditions. The present agricultural landscape was already beginning to emerge as long ago as the twelfth or thirteenth century. Fields were established around dales villages in a growing pattern of arable and pasture land set amidst woodland further up the dale side. However, later enclosure and division of the land was most significant in its effect on the landscape. Small fields and irregular, apparently haphazard, patterns of walls around some villages usually date from enclosures made in the sixteenth century. However, the more regular pattern of field walls on the valley bottoms and the dale sides generally originates from the eighteenth and nineteenth century enclosures, established either by individual schemes or by acts of parliament. The enclosure awards often specified the exact way in which the enclosing walls should be built.

Today, stone wall enclosures are one of the most prominent and characteristic features of the dales landscape. Mile upon mile of wall divides the farm land into many different shapes and sizes of field. The walls mark out the enclosures, often in precise patterns that cut across the contours and help to accentuate the landform. Such effects are particularly pronounced where the walls have been built over the smooth domes of drumlins, as in Teesdale, where the relationship of walls to landform is particularly marked. In the low sun of winter, or in the evening, heavy shadows cast by the walls give even greater definition to these patterns. Views from one dale side to another demonstrate most clearly the mosaic of pasture and walls, and its relationship to farmsteads and woodlands.

The details of wall construction and materials vary widely. Sandstone, old red sandstone and limestone walls all appear in different parts of the area. The shapes and sizes of the stones vary and include thin slabs, square blocks and rounded boulders. Although much of the stone was quarried, a great deal was also cleared from the land. The aim was always to keep to a minimum the distance the stone had to be moved. In a recent study, it was calculated that the field walls in the parish of Lunedale contain about 200,000 tons of stone.

*Notable features of the agricultural landscape are stone walls, field barns, and flower-rich meadows.*

Although the walls are the most striking features of the dales landscape, the fields themselves are also important. They vary in colour and texture, depending on the soil, the way in which the field has been managed, and the time of year. The patterns often accentuate the steps and terraces of the valley slopes. Above the dales, the hill pastures take over, walls decrease in significance, and the patterns of rough grazing and moorland vegetation predominate. Both are agricultural landscapes, but the contrast between the dales and the high moorlands is marked, and is critical to the character of the area. Other important features of the agricultural landscape are droveways, limekilns, field barns and hog-houses.

## Remains of the mining industry

A number of features in the North Pennines landscape date back from the heyday of lead and other mineral mining. The main features and their origins are summarised below.

The majority of ore shoots were vertical, and mining was initially undertaken by the use of vertical shafts. In order to improve accessibility and to drain the mine workings, adit levels (nearly horizontal tunnels) were often used. The large mines used an adit system, which allowed the use of mechanically or horse-drawn wagons to transport the undressed ore or 'bouse' from the working face to the storage area and dressing floor. Most of the vertical shafts are now capped or have collapsed, leaving a visible depression at the surface. Adit levels and drains were often lined with masonry and had arched entrances at the surface. Few of these now remain, with many adit entrances having been deliberately collapsed. Their presence can now only be detected from old wagon-tracks, ponding and wet flushes.

Miners worked in teams or partnerships which were generally responsible for certain parts of the mine or for particular jobs. The bouse worked by these teams had to be stored separately, in order to enable mine agents to calculate the earnings due to each team, and to allow the productivity of each part of the mine to be monitored. The bouse was stored in bays, subdivided by sturdy stone walls, usually in a long, straight line to allow easy access by rail wagon, and often with a facility for overhead tipping. At these 'bousesteads', the first stage of dressing took place – a crude selection of the obvious pieces of ore and waste. Ore was taken to the 'bingstead' and waste to the waste heaps. Many of the stone structures of the bouse and bingsteads still exist, although some have been deliberately ruined or partly dismantled for use as building stone.

Waste heaps were created from the material discarded during the dressing process. Most of this was transported by wagon and tipped, in a 'fan' formation, from a level platform on the hill side. The waste heaps are usually the most visible form of mining disturbance in the landscape today. They are most easily identifiable where they have been left in their original form to grass over, but several of the larger ones have been reworked for other minerals or for crushed stone, and some have been partially cultivated and planted with conifers. Small waste heaps can be found dotted throughout the mining areas, but the most noticeable large-scale waste heaps are in the Rookhope Valley, around Nenthead and at Flushiemere. Waste heaps often support a characteristic flora of lead-tolerant species.

A plentiful supply of water was essential for hydraulic power and for use in the dressing process. Those involved in mining went to great lengths to ensure a constant supply, by interconnecting streams with races, damming existing water courses, and building new reservoirs.

Many of the reservoirs remain intact, sometimes incongruously perched on the hill sides and retained by earth and stone embankments. The most noticeable of these are at Allenheads (Byerhope Reservoir and Dodd Reservoir), Nenthead and Rookhope. The lines of many water races, although dry or partially collapsed, are still visible on the hill sides. 'Hushes' are more dramatic features, and are an important characteristic of the North Pennines mining landscape. Hushes are channels that have been artificially over-deepened by damming, releasing water to scour away the surface-vegetation and soil layer, and exposing the bare rock below. This allowed ore shoots to be identified prior to mining. Hushes appear as gashes in the hill sides, and can usually be identified from a considerable distance.

Water played an important role in the dressing process, as a source of power for crushing machinery and as a hydraulic means of sifting or 'buddling' the crushed ore. This took place on the dressing floor – generally a flat area close to the bousesteads and served by one or more water race. The dressing process was subject to many technological changes, including the switch from hydraulic to steam engines and the use of more sophisticated methods of buddling. There are few remnants of the dressing floor processes and equipment. Only some of the heavier stone structures and the water wheels survive, usually in a ruined state. At the Killhope Lead Mining Museum in Weardale, the water wheel is being restored and is already a significant landmark and tourist attraction.

After the closure of the mines, many of the ancillary buildings were demolished or allowed to go to ruin and used as a source of building stone. In certain locations, the sturdier stone buildings have remained intact. These are usually the workshops, smithy, stables, powder house and occasionally the lodge shop, where miners had temporary accommodation during the working week. At Allenheads and Nenthead, the purpose-built mining villages, the majority of buildings related to mining operations remain intact and many have recently been restored.

Other important structures in the landscape are the smelt mill chimneys, built high on the hill sides to allow the dispersal of noxious fumes at a safe distance away from the nearby village or mining settlement. The main smelt mills were at Nenthead, Allenheads, Allendale and Rookhope, Langley, Dukesfield, and several in the Derwent Valley. The chimneys of many of these mills still stand as prominent features on the skyline, and are connected by long flues to the sites of the smelt mills below. The lines of the underground flues are often not clearly visible and many have suffered collapse along part of their length. As ore had to be carried from numerous locations, a network of carrier ways was developed across the hills. They were used by sturdy ponies pulling wagons, or by workers carrying sacks, depending on the route. Many modern roads follow the routes of carrier ways, while others have become public footpaths. Transport needs also inspired some ambitious railway schemes, most notably the Waskerley Way and rail link to Rookhope, and also rail links to Langley and Allendale and as far as Wearhead. Most of these are now disused, although their lines are clearly visible in the landscape. Interestingly, there is also an underground network of tunnels linking Stanhope with Alston which was used in the severe winter of 1947 to allow movement by doctors on emergency calls.

## Trees, woodlands and forests

Trees and woodlands are not extensive, but they are an extremely important feature of the landscape, helping to create the contrast between the sheltered, green and, in places, well-wooded dales and the wild, open moorlands. In 1890, William Wallace, writing about the parish of Alston Moor (3) noted "a great want of trees to adorn the landscape". This is perhaps surprising, as the London Lead Company were active earlier in the nineteenth century in planting trees to produce timber for use in the mines, as well as to improve the landscape. Plantations and nurseries were planted at remarkably high altitudes, and today much of the timber around Alston originates from this mine planting. Wallace also observed that "the appearance of the country would be greatly improved by planting groups of trees around the farmhouses and upon small patches of waste land". It seems that this advice may have been heeded, because clumps of trees around and near to widely scattered farmsteads are a typical feature of the dales landscape, although many appear to have been planted earlier in the nineteenth century. The clumps are often of sycamore (the plane trees that Wallace recommended) but also include beech and, occasionally, wych elm. These clumps are only one of the many different forms in which trees occur. In the lower dales and on the lower slopes of the middle dales, where climatic conditions are more favourable, there are field and hedgerow trees that can give the landscape a rich well-treed character. They are of many different types, including sycamore, ash, elm and rowan. Occasionally, there are parkland areas of a historic, designed character, with large, free-standing, parkland trees, such as are found at Derwent Grange in Derwentdale and at Whitfield Hall in Lower Allendale.

*Trees and woodlands make an important contribution to the landscape of the dales.*

In addition to the tree clumps that emphasise the farmsteads, the villages in the dales also contribute significantly to tree cover. Despite their relatively high altitude, places like Alston and Allenheads have a remarkable wealth of tree cover around them, providing oases of green in otherwise high, bleak parts of the dales. Much of this planting undoubtedly originated from the activities of the mining companies and other large landowners. Trees in cemeteries and parks, and around public buildings or large houses, contribute most to these settlements. Over the years, planting on old mine workings has also added to the tree cover.

Away from the farmsteads and settlements in the dales, there are occasional isolated tree clumps, such as the highly distinctive landmark of Kirkcarrion, a clump on the site of an ancient tumulus on the hill slopes where Lunedale meets Teesdale, and the 'Elephant Trees', a clump near the watershed south of Stanhope. In the upland fringes, more recent coniferous shelterbelt plantings are common and are characteristic of these marginal areas.

Perhaps the most significant and attractive features in the landscape are the semi-natural and other deciduous woodlands that are usually closely associated with the main rivers and their tributaries. The rivers are generally edged by a band of mature trees, including alder, willow, sycamore, elm, and birch. Where the river has cut steep terraces and embankments, there is usually a swathe of woodland accentuating the slope and the curve of the river, particularly apparent in South Tynedale downstream from Alston, and in Allendale.

The tributaries of the rivers, which cut through the steep dale sides, and are variously known as burns, becks, sikes and ghylls, are often edged by rich, deciduous woodlands. They are sometimes of ancient origin and some are designated Sites of Special Scientific Interest (SSSIs). However, the most significant areas of deciduous woodland occur in the lower stretches of some of the main rivers where they are incised to form steep gorges. Notable examples are the Allen gorges in Lower Allendale, where the Allen passes through a steep gorge around Staward Pele and Plankey Mill, and Lower Derwentdale at Horsleyhope Ravine. Both include diverse deciduous woods which help to create dramatic landscape features. Other notable areas of deciduous woodland occur on the western scarp, particularly Hellbeck and Swindale Woods, which combine with complex limestone geology and broken scarp topography to create unusual and dramatic scenery. In a number of places, there are birch woodlands that sometimes appear to have been grazed out, so that they take on an almost parkland character. A number of birch woods occur in Teesdale and in Derwentdale.

Throughout the North Pennines, there are numerous, fairly small forestry plantations, usually of coniferous species. The boundaries of the AONB were drawn to exclude the large plantations of Slaley and Hamsterley Forests, although the edges of both are visible for some distance. Extensive afforestation of the moorland areas has,

to date, been limited. The plantations that do exist are generally relatively inconspicuous, although many suffer from unfortunate geometric shapes and straight edges. Significant planting has taken place in some dale head areas, notably in Upper Weardale at Killhope and at Allenheads, perhaps because of their more sheltered nature and the marginal character of the land. The dark masses of the forests here appear in stark contrast to the surrounding moorlands.

These many different types of trees and woodlands combine together in some of the dales to give a surprisingly well-wooded feel to the landscape. This is particularly apparent in the lower parts of Teesdale and Weardale, their lower lying tributaries such as the valley of the Waskerley Beck, in South Tynedale and in lower Allendale.

*Water is a very significant feature of the dales landscape, occurring as fast-flowing upland rivers, such as the South Tyne (above left); as dramatic waterfalls, such as at Low Force (below left); and as reservoirs, such as Cow Green Reservoir (below).*

# 3. Variations in landscape character

There are considerable variations in the character of the North Pennines landscape. This means that, while the whole area has a strong regional identity and is clearly a single landscape unit, there are a number of distinct types of landscape within it, each with its own particular range of characteristics.

In simple terms, the North Pennines can be divided into four main types of landscape, namely moorlands, dales, upland fringes and the western scarp. Almost everyone would recognise the differences between these types, and it is these contrasts that help to make the North Pennines such a special area. There are, however, even more subtle variations within these types that give great diversity to the landscape. The distribution of the full range of landscape types is shown in Figure 4 (overleaf), and the character of each is described below.

## Moorland landscapes

To many people, it is the high moorlands that are the epitome of the North Pennines landscape. Ridges of moorland form the watersheds dividing the dales. They are high,

generally lying above 450 metres, and apparently remote, with a severe climate. The landform is generally rolling, with convex slopes, but there are also broad plateaux and basins. Many areas are covered by a thick layer of peat, but in places the underlying rock is exposed, forming scars, scree and rock bands, and providing a marked contrast in colour and texture with the surrounding moorland.

It is the vegetation of these moorland areas that gives them so much of their character. Heather is perhaps the most common, but there are many different types of moorland, with cotton grass and bilberry also widespread, and grass moorland, with mat grass and bents and *fescues*, appearing where grazing pressure is heavy.

The contrasts in colour between these different types of vegetation, especially between the dark heather, the light, sometimes white, grassland, and the bright green flashes of bilberry, is particularly characteristic. There are also striking seasonal changes, notably the flowering of the heather, the changing shades of green grassland, and the bronze shades of bracken in some areas. In addition to variations in vegetation, much of the interest of these areas lies in patterns on the land – patterns of exposed stone, of eroding peat edges, of gullies and gills, hummocks and hollows, both natural and man made, as well as the patchwork that results from heather burning.

Most of the moorland landscapes are typified by uninterrupted views, by their wild character, by their apparent, if not actual, naturalness, by their extent and uniformity, as well as by the subtleties of colour, texture and pattern described above. The lack of visible, man-made features is a notable characteristic of much of the moorland. These features are common to all of these landscapes, but there are distinctly different areas.

## Moorland ridges

The main dales in the eastern half of the AONB are divided by ridges of moorland that extend out in fingers from the high watershed to the west. These ridges consist of a series of gently rolling summits, rising up to 700 metres in the west and to 450–500 metres in the east. These ridges tend to be generally drier, with much less prominent peat deposits, and a more uniform dry heath type of vegetation. Burning patterns are often prominent, but otherwise the only incidents in the otherwise horizontal landscape are grazing sheep and occasional lines of fence posts. Because the ridges are relatively narrow, the extent of unbroken moorland views is limited, compared with the higher moorland summits to the west, and there are often long views over a sequence of ridges, with dales partly visible in-between. This reduces the feeling of remoteness and unbroken extent, but provides added interest.

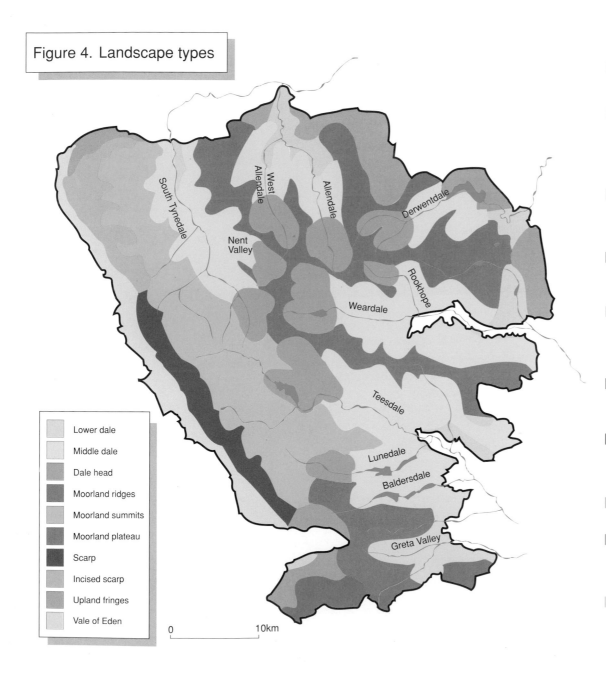

## Figure 4. Landscape types

**Legend:**
- Lower dale
- Middle dale
- Dale head
- Moorland ridges
- Moorland summits
- Moorland plateau
- Scarp
- Incised scarp
- Upland fringes
- Vale of Eden

0      10km

**Map labels:** South Tynedale, West Allendale, Allendale, Derwentdale, Nent Valley, Rookhope, Weardale, Teesdale, Lunedale, Baldersdale, Greta Valley

## Summary of landscape features

### Lower dale
Enclosed, intimate character; deciduous woodlands on valley sides; strong field patterns; dense tree cover with hedgerows, hedgerow trees, copses and woodlands.

### Middle dale
Complexity and diversity; rich pattern of textures and colours; sense of historical continuity; flower-rich valley bottom meadows and pastures; strong pattern of stone walls; scattered farmsteads with clumps; field trees along stone walls; vernacular style of stone buildings and settlements; tree-lined river landscapes; dale-side ghylls and woodland; contrasting colours of moorland fringe; evidence of mining history including high level farmsteads; stepped landform.

### Dale head
Shallow, even gradient of valley sides; deeply incised becks; uninterrupted encircling moorland skyline; marginal character; cultivation, enclosure and settlement at their limits; reverting, rush-infested pastures; derelict walls and buildings; mining remains; forestry plantations; bleak character.

### Moorland ridges
Apparent naturalness and lack of human influence; gently rolling ridges and summits; uniform dry heath vegetation; colours and patterns of heather; prominent burning patterns; uninterrupted extent; views over sequences of dales and moorland.

### Moorland summits
Wild, remote character; severe climate; extent and uniformity of blanket bog vegetation; openness and apparent naturalness; relative lack of man-made structures and human influence; landform of sweeping interlocking ridges; prominent and distinctive millstone grit caps on high summits; dramatic distant views; patterns on the land; peat haggs; hidden valleys of becks.

### Moorland plateau
Relatively flat and featureless topography; apparent naturalness; lack of human influence; continuous blanket peat bog; bleak, wilderness character; lack of landmarks; upstanding, rocky band of Shackleborough.

### Scarp
Dramatic landforms; outlying conical hills; unbroken sweep of unimproved rough grazing; colour contrasts between different types of grassland; exposed rock features; lack of enclosure except on lower slopes; bare, treeless character; long views out to Vale of Eden and beyond; prominence in views from the west; dramatic lighting effects of low sun.

### Incised scarp
As above but more gentle slopes; complex topography with incised valleys, outlying hills and a secondary escarpment.

### Upland fringes
Gently rolling or terraced landform; small valleys; enclosed pasture; some arable land; mixed field boundaries of fences, hedges and walls; prominent farmsteads; large farm buildings; coniferous shelterbelts; sycamore clumps. Limestone fringe in the south west is distinct.

### Vale of Eden
Rich, diverse character; complex, rolling drumlin topography; rich, red soils; pasture and arable fields; red sandstone villages often with village green; dense network of tree-lined lanes, small, wooded valleys and hedgerows with trees.

## Moorland summits

Above the Vale of Eden and the western scarp, the tilt of the Alston Block has created a ridge of high moorland summits. This ridge contains the highest summits in the whole Pennine chain, with a number of them, notably Mickle Fell, Meldon Hill, Knock Fell, Great Dun Fell, Little Dun Fell and Cross Fell, rising to more than 750 metres in height, and the highest, Cross Fell, at 893 metres, being the highest Pennine summit. From these heights, the ridge falls away in a series of summits of generally decreasing height, to the north towards the King's Forest of Geltsdale and Cold Fell, and to the south towards Lunedale.

This summit ridge is the heart of the North Pennine uplands. It is an extremely wild and remote area, crossed by only two roads throughout its 45-kilometre length. The landform is one of sweeping and interlocking ridges, with the Millstone Grit caps that form the highest fells standing out with their stepped profiles and flat tops. The flanks of the ridges are cut by a number of burns or sikes, creating hidden valleys, with silvery ribbons of water snaking through the surrounding moorlands. The valley of the Black Burn, clearly visible from the Hartside road, is an outstanding example of such a valley. The Maize Beck is another, although it is much more accessible because of its position on the route of the Pennine Way.

*The landscape of the moorland summits is characterised by its extensive, wild, remote character and by its severe climate and apparent naturalness.*

Peat covers much of the ridge, and forms extensive blanket bog, with heather and cotton grass creating a mosaic of colour and dark peat haggs often breaking the surface. Grey stones punctuate the moorland in many places, and form grey bands around the highest summits. They have been used to build cairns, which are often the only vertical accents in the sweeps of horizontal moorland.

The summits have an extremely severe climate, with high levels of rain and snowfall, low temperatures and extreme winds. The infamous local wind, known as the 'helm' wind (the only wind in Britain to have a name), originates on these summits and occasionally wreaks havoc in the Vale of Eden below. The average summer temperature at Cow Green Reservoir is said to be the same as at Rekjavik in Iceland. Such extreme conditions can combine to make these moorlands bleak and forbidding, and the summits are often wreathed in cloud and mist. However, when the cloud does lift and the sun comes through, the landscape is transformed. Dramatic views open up from the summits, over the dales to the east and, most dramatically, over the Vale of Eden to the west and beyond to the Lake District.

The overriding impression is one of a natural landscape where there is little sign of the hand of man. However, there are notable exceptions to this, particularly the radar station on Great Dun Fell. The buildings, white dome, and other trappings are visible for miles around. There are also signs of man's influence in the remains of the mining industry, which reached even to these great heights. There are relics of shafts, levels and hushes, with a particularly prominent one near Great Dun Fell. Nevertheless, despite these influences, and recognising that it is agricultural management that maintains the moorland landscape, these moorland summits must rank as the greatest area of upland wilderness in England.

### Moorland plateau

From Lunedale and the B6726 road that crosses the summit ridge, south almost to the boundary of the Yorkshire Dales National Park, there is an extensive area of essentially flat moorland plateau lying across the Stainmore depression. Although this area has many of the features of the other moorland landscapes, it is distinguished by its lower altitude of 400–500 metres, the relatively flat and featureless topography, the almost continuous blanket peat bog, and its bleak character.

One of the few notable landmarks is the upstanding rocky band of Shackleborough, visible over some distance. Although the landscape is in fact a series of low parallel ridges running from west to east, much of the lower ground is hidden from view, creating a uniform appearance. Wainwright, in describing the stretch of the Pennine Way that passes the northern half of this area, described it as "the greatest wilderness in the country ....a no-man's land, ....little known and rarely visited ....that has no roads and no paths and no landmarks ....an upland desert".

## Dales landscapes

The dales offer a complete contrast with the moorland landscapes, being enclosed, sheltered, settled and domestic. Each dale demonstrates a number of transitions in character, based on changes in altitude.

Taking an average cross-section of the dale, there are changes in altitude from 280 metres in the valley bottom to perhaps 450 metres at the enclosing view line. The river course itself, often edged by a woodland band, runs through the valley bottom, which is either flat on river alluvium, gravels or boulder-clay deposits, or rolling where there are drumlins. This area supports better quality in-bye meadows and pasture, and contains many of the farms, villages and roads. Above this, the valley sides slope up steeply, covered by a pattern of walls, pastures, and small woodlands and containing the higher level farms and settlements, often of mining origin. Above this again, there are the larger, walled allotments that were formed by enclosure of moorland, and then the moorland fringes, spreading down into the dales from the moorland ridges above.

Taking the long section, from the head of the valley where the rivers rise, to the point where they leave the upland block, there are similar changes in altitude but over much greater distances. For example, Teesdale starts at about 550 metres, at the head of Harwood Beck, and falls to about 220 metres below Middleton-in-Teesdale. This produces a gradual transition from moorland, through rough, upland pastures, to better quality agricultural land. The effects of these changes in altitude upon vegetation patterns, agricultural and game management and settlement patterns, produce distinct variations in landscape character, creating three broad types, namely dale head, middle and lower dale landscapes.

### Dale heads

These landscapes are the broad basins that occur at the head of each dale, where the becks and burns which feed the river flow off the fells and converge to form the larger headwaters of the river. They generally occur high in the moorland core, at altitudes of 400–500 metres, and are characterised by the shallow, even gradient of the valley sides, a pronounced, encircling moorland skyline, and deep gullying caused by the eroding action of the becks. Cultivation, enclosure and settlement have been pushed to their limits in many of these areas, often reflecting the mining history of the area when miner–farmers established small-holdings and cultivated land at this level in the valleys.

*Teesdale clearly demonstrates the complexity and diversity of these landscapes.*

*Stone walls, and the shadows that they cast, help to accentuate the landform.*

*Lower down the dales, deciduous woodlands are notable features in the landscape, here combined with a reservoir in the valley of the Waskerley Beck.*

The marginal nature of farming in these areas means that there is a constant tendency for enclosed allotments and pastures to revert to moorland, and for farmsteads and outbuildings to be abandoned. Pastures are often rush-infested, with walls and buildings tending to dereliction, sometimes creating a bleak, unsettling landscape. Perhaps because these areas are marginal, and also because they are a little more sheltered than the surrounding moors, there has been significant afforestation in some dale heads, notably Upper Weardale and around Allenheads.

## Middle dales

It is in the middle sections of the dales that perhaps the most typical Pennine dales landscape is found. Usually, there is a strong, clearly defined river channel, marked by a bank of riverside trees and woodlands. This creates a small-scale river landscape with its own particular qualities, based on the rocky upland character of the rivers, with waterfalls, rapids, riffles and still pools, with tree-lined, steep banks, and with road and foot bridges as special features.

The valley bottom is a landscape of flat or rolling walled meadows and pastures, which produce a carpet of flowers in the spring and early summer. The stone walls are often punctuated by lines of trees, and by barns and farmsteads. Villages and farmsteads built in the local vernacular style nestle just above the flood plain, linked by roads running along the valley with occasional cross-links from side to side.

The steeply sloping valley sides are characterised by a great diversity of features. The stepped profile formed by the alternating shales, sandstone and limestone of the Yoredale series is often visible. The shales weather more, and so form flatter terraces, which are accentuated by changes in the colour and texture of grassland. A network of regular stone walls imposes a strong pattern on the landform, and farms and settlements spread high up the valley sides. Field trees follow the walls, and clumps of sycamore mark the positions of buildings. Tributary becks are incised steeply into the dale sides, sometimes forming waterfalls where they pass over harder rock bands, and deciduous woodlands mark their course. Higher up, field sizes increase, the grazing becomes rougher, and the skyline is formed by the moorland fringe, appearing green in the summer, tinged with purple in the autumn, and olive-gold or almost white as the grasses wither in the winter.

These landscapes are complex and diverse. There is always something to catch the eye, and there are rich patterns and textures at many different levels – the textures and colours of flowers carpeting the meadows, the patterns of the stone walls, and the varying shades of the fields on the valley side. There is a strong sense of historical continuity and of the maintenance of traditional land management. Buildings and settlements, with their vernacular stone character, give a satisfying unity to the landscape, and the scattered remains of mining activity provide a reminder of the traditions that have helped to shape it.

## Lower dales

The lower dales landscape occurs at the fringes of the area, where the dales pass out of the upland area and open into broader valleys. The lower altitudes allow more intensive agriculture, and hedgerows largely replace stone walls. Tree cover is denser than in the middle dales and includes hedgerows, hedgerow trees, riverside trees, copses, and woodlands. Field patterns are strong and the landscapes have an enclosed and intimate feel that is comfortable and familiar to many people, especially when compared with the high moorlands.

Deciduous woodlands play an important role in these landscapes, on valley sides and on river terraces. Where the rivers are deeply incised in gorges, as they leave the uplands, there are extensive areas of valley woodland forming a quite distinctive and very picturesque landscape.

Although this general pattern of variation is repeated in all of the dales, differences in geology, topography and land use history make every dale different. It would not do justice to the great variety of dales landscapes to settle for these generalised descriptions, so the distinctive features of each of the main dales are set out opposite.

# Teesdale

This is perhaps the best known of the dales, famous for its rare and unusual flora which is recognised by the designation of large areas as National Nature Reserve. It provides some of the most varied, interesting and attractive landscapes in the AONB, and is among the most popular areas for visitors. On a sunny day in early summer, it is without doubt an outstandingly beautiful landscape. Running in a south easterly direction, Teesdale is a long, broad dale with several substantial tributaries joining it in the south east. Outcrops of Whin Sill quartz dolerite are common, and form a series of notable and spectacular features, including cliffs, scars and waterfalls.

The lower dale, which is a rich pastoral landscape with numerous hedgerows and hedgerow trees, has been largely excluded from the AONB. The middle dale demonstrates many of the classic features of Pennine dales landscapes, with a complex pattern of stone walls, meadows and pastures. On the valley floor, the walls, many of them built of rounded stones, cut across the gentle domes of a series of drumlins, accentuating the landform. The south western side of the dale is formed by the lower flanks of the moorland summit ridge and by bands of the Whin Sill that outcrop along it, forming the dark cliffs of Holwick Scar. The north eastern face has occasional light outcrops of limestone, which stand out in contrast to the surrounding rough limestone grassland and the enclosed dale-side pastures.

Most of the land in the dale north of the river is owned by the Raby estate. All of the estate farms are painted white, and these white buildings are prominent throughout the dale. The River Tees is at its most spectacular in this middle section. Below Forest-in-Teesdale, it cuts through low, rocky hills, some covered in the dark green of rare juniper scrub, and over the spectacular, high and foaming waterfall of High Force, formed by an erosion resistant band of the Whin Sill. High Force has attracted visitors for nearly two hundred years, and the walk to it still retains much of the feel of a Victorian beauty spot. Further down the valley, the river meanders through a broader flood plain, but further Whin Sill bands create the less dramatic but still picturesque waterfall of Low Force. Flower-rich meadows are plentiful alongside the river, and throughout this stretch of the dale there is a wealth of interest and beauty.

The dale head is extensive and open, dividing into two distinct parts. The true head of the Tees itself penetrates high into the moorland summit ridge. It is an uncultivated moorland landscape in which Whin Sill features are prominent.

Cronkley Scar and Falcon Clints are dark cliffs of dolerite columns, broken stone blocks and dark heather, contrasting with the bright colours of bracken and occasional trees clinging to the rocks. Cauldron Snout is another dramatic waterfall which allows the Tees to drop in rocky steps to a lower level. Above this, the dale head is dominated by the shining water of Cow Green Reservoir, formed, very controversially, by damming the Tees. Although the dam and associated structures are intrusions in a wild landscape, the bright sheet of water they retain provides a contrasting element in the bleak moorland landscape, and is regarded by many as having its own charm.

The other more typical dale head is formed by the headwaters of the Harwood Beck which joins the Tees at Forest-in-Teesdale. It is broad and open and virtually treeless, with grass moorland swooping down to quite low levels before stone walls and allotments appear. Unlike some of the other dale heads, there is less evidence of lead mining history here, and less of an impression of abandonment or neglect. The undulating plain of Widdybank Fell, with its rich and varied flora, divides the Harwood Beck from the Tees. In such an open landscape, the numerous, scattered, white-painted farmsteads are a striking and distinctive feature.

## Lunedale, Baldersdale and the Greta Valley

These dales are significant tributary valleys to Teesdale. All share the same basic pattern of dale head, middle and lower dale landscapes but vary in their individual characteristics.

**Lunedale** is dominated by Grassholme and Selset Reservoirs. The topography around them is varied and complex – undulating in the lower valley, more consistently sloping in the middle section, and deeply dissected in the valley head. The valley sides are predominantly stone wall enclosed pastures, but there are forestry plantations and mixed woodlands around the reservoir. The tree clump on the ancient tumulus of Kirkcarrion is a prominent landscape feature high on a bluff between Baldersdale and Teesdale. There are also a number of disused and active quarries and there is active fluorspar mining.

**Baldersdale** runs parallel to Lunedale, to the south east, and is very similar in character, containing Hury, Blackton and Balderhead Reservoirs. It is a quite shallow valley with simple, undramatic convex green hills, large, walled pastures and scattered farmsteads. It is best known as the former home of Hannah Hauxwell, the solitary dales-woman of television fame, but is otherwise remote, although crossed by the route of the Pennine Way.

**The Greta Valley** in the Stainmore Gap alongside the A66, is the southernmost valley in the area, joined to the west by the significant tributary of Sleightholme Beck. Both are notable for unusual limestone features – the limestone arch of God's Bridge on the Greta and the Sleightholme Beck gorge. The Greta Valley is broad with gently sloping sides, and a terraced form. There are large, walled enclosures, some rough and tussocky with invading rushes, some green and lush with field trees. High moorland ridges to the south form intermediate and distant skylines. The A66 runs along the top of the valley to the north and introduces a number of intrusive features, including the noise and fumes from the heavy traffic, electricity lines, and various roadside facilities. The head of the valley is long, narrow and shallow, with tributary watercourses deeply incised into moorland.

# Weardale

Commonly known as 'the lead dale', Weardale is a long east–west valley, like Teesdale, although generally narrower and with none of the dramatic Whin Sill landscape features. It demonstrates the typical range of dales landscapes, but is distinguished by its significant mining and quarrying history and the widespread legacy of lead mining in the landscape.

Much of the lower dale was excluded from the AONB after the public inquiry, because of the effects of quarrying and related industry. However, the side valley of the Waskerley Beck, north of Wolsingham, demonstrates many of the lower dale characteristics, lying generally below 300 metres. It has good tree cover, with a mixture of field trees, overgrown hedgerows, garden trees and woods, creating a lush and enclosed landscape. Although not typical of the lower Weardale landscape, Tunstall Reservoir occupies the centre of the Waskerley Beck Valley and has some ecologically important and very attractive ancient deciduous woodlands on its flanks. There are also some fine stone buildings in the valley, including some related to the reservoir.

The middle part of the dale has all of the characteristic landscape features. The pattern of valley-bottom meadows is complex, and interspersed with woodland on river terraces. On the valley sides, the fields are often small and rectangular, with the walls accentuating the stepped landform. Some of them are of prehistoric origin. The settlements in the dale bottom form an almost continuous ribbon of development, and there are widespread signs of former lead mining, including hushes, mine buildings and spoil heaps. Numerous tributaries cut down deeply into the valley sides, forming steep V-shaped gullies, with deciduous woodland clinging to their sides.

West beyond Cowshill, the dale head begins and has a clearly distinct character. The flat valley-bottom land disappears and the dale at first narrows then opens into a broad basin where the Killhope and Wellhope burns join to form the Wear. Lead mining has had a profound influence on the landscape, and one of the best preserved mine sites, including a substantial and famous water wheel, lies at the heart of the dale head. It has now been opened to interpret the history of the industry to the public. Miner-farmers settled high up in this dale head, but much of the enclosed grazing land that they farmed has now been more or less abandoned, leaving derelict walls and barns, rush-infested pastures and a sometimes depressing air of neglect. Coniferous plantations have been established in blocks on some of the higher slopes. Their dark regular shapes form a stark contrast with the surrounding moorland pastures, but the lower edges create sheltered and enclosed spaces in an otherwise somewhat bleak landscape.

Rookhope is an important tributary valley running into the Wear from the north. The lower part, below the village of Rookhope itself, is much like the middle section of Weardale, although on a smaller scale. The burn itself is cut down into a narrow, deep, often wooded gorge-like valley. The slopes above have a regular pattern of square stone walls, with only a few scattered trees and some farmsteads and barns. Above Rookhope, the character of the landscape changes and becomes akin to an elongated dale head. Here the landscape is open and largely treeless. The river meanders through a narrower open floodplain, and the terraced dale sides are made up of large walled enclosures, containing rush-infested pastures and open grass moorland, and dissected by gullies. Lead mining has had a major effect on the landscape, and the physical remnants are often highly visible. There are hushes and spoil banks all along the slopes, all sorts of shafts, and the eye-catching and much photographed stone archway which once carried the Rookhope chimney, designed to carry fumes from smelters high up the valley side. Two fluorspar mines add to the industrial feel of the valley, which is in marked contrast with the wild moorland ridges beyond. The somewhat bleak character of the valley is heightened by the presence of power-lines, fences and a scattering of unsightly sheep-sheds.

# Allendale and West Allendale

These twin dales run from south to north and are cut respectively by the Rivers East and West Allen. Both are relatively short, running some 16 kilometres from the dale head to the point where they join to form the River Allen. They drop quite quickly in this distance and, although the upper parts are high and enclosed, the valleys soon open out to become broad and shallow, again clearly demonstrating the asymmetrical cross section. Moorland grazing, often heather-dominated common land, but also more heavily grazed grass moorland, forms a prominent skyline in the upper and middle dales. Although walls are still a feature of the dales, the patterns are not as marked as in Teesdale and Weardale, and there is little evidence of limestone influences on the landscape. The dales have more of a gritstone upland character and valley-side woodlands and shelterbelts, which tend to be more prominent than the field pattern, give the landscape a character which echoes the landscapes lying north of the Tyne Gap. Lead mining has had a major effect on the landscape of both dales, especially in the dale heads where, as in Nentdale, Rookhope and Weardale, there are many mining remains.

**Allendale** itself has an extensive dale head ringed by an almost circular skyline of high moorland and with the purpose-built mining village of Allenheads nestling at its centre. There has been extensive forestry planting all around the village, often on mine waste, but also on abandoned pastures and moorland slopes. Planting near the village has given it a distinctive skyline of contrasting dark conifers and light green deciduous trees. Isolated farmsteads and small settlements are scattered throughout the dale head and down to Spartylea and Sinderhope – evidence of the miner–farmers small-holdings. There is evidence of former mine-working throughout the area.

Further down the valley, deciduous woodland, conifer plantations and shelterbelts are a prominent feature. As in South Tynedale, the eastern flank has a prominent steep and colourful bluff of heather and bracken, here formed by Allendale Common, which is cut into by the narrow and enticing moorland valley of Sipton Cleugh. Quite quickly there is a transition to the lower dale landscape. The valley becomes broader and shallower, moorland fringes disappear and green pastures spread right over the watershed. Hedges replace walls, although the two often appear together, and river terrace woodlands become increasingly prominent as the East Allen reaches its confluence with the West Allen.

**West Allendale** is distinguished firstly by its bleak, open dale head with steeply sloping sides of rough grazing, and plentiful evidence of another abandoned lead mining area around Coalcleugh. It now has an empty, neglected character, half-way between the wild moorlands above and the more lush, settled parts of the valley beyond. To the north, the middle dale has gently sloping, gullied sides with prominent woodlands, geometric coniferous shelterbelts and hedges mixed with the walls.

It is in the lower dale that West Allendale is so different in character. Below Carr's Beck, the influence of the eighteenth century Whitfield Hall and its estate creates a landscape of parkland and pleasure grounds, thick plantations and steep, deciduous valley woodlands. It is a well tended, sheltered and picturesque landscape, and seems another world from the bleak dale head only a short distance away.

Beyond the confluence of the Rivers East and West Allen, the River Allen cuts deeply down to form a gorge in the surrounding uplands, creating, with its tributaries, an extensive landscape of deep, thickly wooded river gorges. This is a well-known beauty spot, with popular woodland and riverside walks accessible from places such as Plankey Mill and Ridley. Viewed from the plateau above, heavily wooded ridges recede into the distance along the valley. Down in the gorge, the river itself is rocky, with some beaches offering access to the water, and suspension foot-bridges providing vantage points. Thick, deciduous woodlands tower above on the valley sides, creating an extremely picturesque landscape that is ideally suited to recreation.

# South Tynedale

This the longest of the north–south dales, extending 24 kilometres from Tyne head to the Lambley viaduct. It has the typical asymmetrical cross section of the north–south dales, with steeply sloping valley sides to the east and gentle slopes to the west, running up to the northern part of the high moorland ridge. Williamston Common forms a particularly prominent feature to the east of the river, partly because of its steepness, but also because unimproved heather and bracken slopes spill right down towards the river, catching the eye, particularly when the bracken has turned to russet. Elsewhere, the stepped form of the valley sides is particularly prominent, and the hill fort of Whitley Castle, with its irregular profile, is an important landmark.

The dale head is typical, with rough allotments intermixed with grass moorland, although there are few farms. The middle dale landscape is extensive, with large, stone-walled enclosures of relatively poor, often rush-infested pastures on the gentle moorland flanks to the west, and steeper, usually smaller enclosures to the east. The dale is notable for extensive tree and woodland cover. Prominent deciduous woodlands run parallel to the river on terraces, emphasising the meandering river course. Steep woods follow the small tributaries down the valley sides, and there is extensive mixed woodland in the northern part of the valley, clothing much of the valley sides. Around Alston, a mixture of field trees, trees in large gardens and around public buildings, and woods and forestry plantations on the valley sides, give the town a green and sheltered character that is quite unexpected given its location at over 300 metres in height. North of Alston, the River South Tyne itself meanders through broad, flat, alluvial pastures and is edged by a varied band of deciduous trees and by areas of rich, damp grassland. A series of old, river terraces contribute to quite complex topography on the valley floor. The field pattern is less dominant than in Teesdale and Weardale, and woods on river terraces are a prominent feature. The northern section, below Lambley viaduct, is characterised by extensive stretches of mixed woodland on the middle slopes of the dale side, enclosing broad sweeps of alluvial meadow alongside the meandering river.

The Nent Valley is formed by the main tributary of the South Tyne and is distinguished by the effects of lead mining. Nenthead, in the dale head, is one of the high settlements created by the mining industry. There is widespread and clearly apparent evidence of mining history all around the area, including spoil heaps, mine buildings, dwellings, levels, shafts, lagoons and hushes. The village has a feeling of abandonment and dereliction, but is of considerable historical interest. Many of the pastures, improved by the miner-farmers, have reverted to rush-infested marginal moorland, and walls, barns and farmsteads have been abandoned.

# Derwentdale

Lying in the north eastern corner of the North Pennines, Derwentdale is quite unlike the other dales, lacking many of the characteristics of typical Pennine dales. It is generally of lower altitudes, running from 500 metres at its head to below 200 metres in the lower reaches. The enclosing moorland ridges are generally only 300–400 metres high. The dale head is split into two elongated sections formed by the Boldon and Nookton burns high up in the moorland and quickly turning to long, narrow and heavily wooded valleys around Hunstanworth. They are secluded and intimate with no road access.

The middle dale, from Hunstanworth eastwards, is in two parts. Firstly, there is the extremely attractive 'estate' landscape around Blanchland and Hunstanworth, both of them picturesque, designed estate villages set in a landscape of wooded valleys. Below this the dale is occupied by the Derwent Reservoir. A wide expanse of water fills most of the dale, with low enclosing sides, lush, green pastures and a dense pattern of woodlands and shelterbelts. Birch woodlands and dark coniferous shelterbelts are prominent and occasional bands of gorse provide accents of colour when in flower.

Below the reservoir, the valley is closed off by the green wall of the dam, the Derwent reappears and fields are enclosed by gappy hedgerows which have grown up to form lines of small hedgerow trees. The valley then cuts down deeply in the lower dale to form a heavily wooded gorge system similar to that on the lower reaches of the Allen. The upper slopes are an intimate mix of woodland, small pastures, overgrown hedges and field trees, creating a small-scale, diverse and domestic landscape. Within the gorge and valley system, thick, rich mixed deciduous woodlands cling to steep valley sides, enclosing the Derwent and its tributaries and occasionally wrapping around small, isolated areas of riverside pasture. This is a secret landscape of shelter and enclosure, rich wildlife and the sights and sounds of the river.

## Scarp landscapes and the Vale of Eden

These landscape types are described together because of the close interrelationships between them. The scarp landscape runs in a broad band along the western edge of the AONB. It is a dramatic escarpment falling away, often precipitously, to the Vale of Eden at its foot, and is characterised particularly by the inspiring views it provides westwards over the vale, and beyond to the prominent skyline of the Lake District fells. Viewed from below, it forms an imposing unbroken wall above the vale, visible from the A66 and the M6. Its orientation means that low, evening sunshine and sunsets can produce spectacular lighting effects, especially when white winter grassland on the scarp is illuminated against cloudy skies. This may explain why Defoe, writing about his travels in the area, describes it as a "wall of brass". Weather and lighting effects also play an important part in views from the scarp and the moorland summits beyond. It is common for grey, cloudy skies to break above the Vale of Eden, and for isolated shafts of sunlight to throw a spotlight on the fertile patchwork of fields below.

There are two types of scarp landscape. The southern scarp below the pass at Hartside is high, steep and apparently unbroken for much of its length. The moorland summits above form a secondary skyline beyond the scarp itself. The scarp face is covered in the main by unimproved rough grazing, with the types and colours of grassland varying according to the underlying geology. There are areas of acid grassland with mat grass and *fescue*, short bright green, limestone grassland with some limestone pavement, and occasional patches of heather. On the scarp foothills, large walled enclosures of improved grazing creep up to the limits of cultivation, and some areas have been planted for forestry.

Bands of rock break through to form horizontal scars of limestone and dolerite. These scars occur in places along the length of the scarp slope but are most pronounced in the extreme south above Brough, where they form extremely complex exposures. This is the point where the Pennine fault meets the more southerly Dent fault, causing great disturbance to the layers of rock. Passing through the rock bands, for example in descending the Pennine Way to Dufton, there are sometimes small-scale landscapes of hummocky, rocky 'badlands', forming enclosed spaces among low hills.

The scarp face appears to be unbroken, but it is gullied by short, steep becks and gills, rising on the moorland ridge and running down eventually to join the Eden. They do no more than furrow the surface, but below Dufton Fell the scarp topography is complex and broken, creating some spectacular scenery. Most dramatically, the scarp is severed by the awesome slash of High Cup with its Whin Sill cliffs, sweeping slopes, screes, and silver ribbon of water. Although it is less impressive, the valley of the Hilton Beck, just to the south, is also a deep incision into the scarp.

The underlying geology becomes more complex below these features. Older slates and volcanic rocks are exposed between the carboniferous rocks and the red sandstone of the Vale of Eden, and form the outlying conical hills of Dufton and Knock Pikes, creating a varied landscape of steep slopes, deep valleys, and pointed summits.

The northern scarp is deeply incised, generally lower and more gentle in landform. It has fewer crags and screes, and drops more gradually to the Vale of Eden. The northernmost part is complex, with the scarp incised by the long valleys of Croglin Water and the wooded Geltsdale. There are rounded, outlying hills in Cumrew and Talkin Fells, and a secondary escarpment is formed by the steep slopes below Cold Fell, wrapping around to the north almost to the entry to South Tynedale.

The Vale of Eden, lying between the scarp and the Lake District is, as its name suggests, a rich and bountiful landscape. At close quarters it is a valley of complex glacial landforms, with long, whaleback drumlins, rich red soils formed from the underlying red sandstone, productive pastures and arable fields, a network of hedges, trees, narrow tree-lined lanes, and wooded stream valleys, and farms and villages, built in red sandstone, which seem to grow from the land around them. Viewed from above, the Vale is seen as a chequerboard of fields of different colours and sizes, broken by a maze of hedges and roads, and dotted with mature trees. The diversity and richness of

*The western scarp gives dramatic views over the Vale of Eden to the Lakeland fells.*

the landscape is uplifting to the spirits when it is suddenly revealed after crossing the moors at Hartside, or the Stainmore Gap, or emerging at the head of High Cup on the Pennine Way.

Most of the Vale of Eden lies outside the AONB, not because it is considered to be inferior in its natural beauty, but because it is not part of the North Pennines as such. However, the foothills, where the Vale runs up to join the scarp, are included, together with the string of fell-foot, red sandstone villages strung along the bottom of the escarpment. Although very much a part of the Vale of Eden, these villages, including Dufton, Knock, Melmerby and Newbiggin, are closely linked to the scarp above, agriculturally, administratively through their parish boundaries, and as inseparable parts of the landscape. These scarp-foot villages are gems of rural townscape. Many have village greens, some have planned layouts, while others are delightfully informal.

*Viewed from below, the scarp is a striking feature, especially when lit by low evening or winter sun.*

*At the foot of the scarp nestle a string of red sandstone villages, often built, as shown here at Dufton, around a village green.*

## Upland fringes

Around the edges of the area are a number of places that do not exhibit the characteristic features of moorland landscapes, of dales, or even of the scarp. They lie at the fringes of the area, primarily along the northern and eastern edges, and consist of gently rolling upland landscapes of low ridges and hills, dissected by small, often wooded valleys. They lie below 300 metres and, as a result, are predominantly enclosed grassland rather than moorland, although some patches of moorland and heath vegetation remain. Because of the more favourable conditions at this lower altitude, farming is more intensive than in the higher parts of the AONB. Although grazing still predominates, there is arable land in the extreme east, alongside the A68. Field boundaries are a mixture of walls, post and wire fences, and some gappy hedges and hedgerow trees. Gorse, in roadside hedges, on rough uncultivated banks and alongside streams, provides a flash of colour. Farmsteads tend to be prominent in the open landscape and often include large, new buildings. Clumps of sycamores or pines form shelterbelts around them and pine shelterbelts are common. These marginal upland landscapes have few distinctive features and are more typical of a wide area of upland outside the AONB.

A contrasting fringe landscape occurs where the Stainmore Gap drops down from the moorland plateau to the Vale of Eden, at the point where the Pennine and Dent faultlines meet. This is a limestone fringe area that is not truly part of the scarp, lacking its steep incline and striking form, but nevertheless having its own distinctive features. The ground drops away from the uplands above, forming a series of flat terraces with limestone outcrops, exposed, flat pavements and broken topography. There are a number of scattered farmsteads, with better quality grazing on the flat terraces. Steep stream courses, which are headwaters of the River Eden, cut down through the terraces and support rich deciduous woodlands.

## The sequence of landscape types

It will be clear from the number and character of different types of landscape that the area is one of great diversity. Few people experience just one type of landscape, but move instead through a number of different landscapes, either by car or on foot. The unfolding sequence of contrasting scenery is particularly pronounced in the North Pennines because of the often narrow ridges of moorland and the number of dales lying so close together. Any road through the area reveals a series of changing landscapes. Roads along the dales pass through the lower dale, with its more lowland character; the middle dale, with its complex mix of river, walls, meadows, trees, woodlands, farmsteads and upland grazing; the often bleak and neglected landscapes of the dale head; the quite different world of the moors, with their lonely, remote character, the sounds of curlews and golden plovers, and miles of often unbroken moorland vegetation; before dropping from the tops to the next dale, or over the scarp to the wonders of the Vale of Eden. Roads that cut across the dales pass through this sequence in a shorter distance, from the river, up through the walled enclosures of the daleside, the more marginal allotments, and out onto the heather moors, but with glimpses of the next dale beyond appearing quite quickly. The sequence then begins again as the road passes down to the next river, then up once more.

Walkers on the many footpaths in the area are able to appreciate the subtleties of change in the landscape and to enjoy the smaller features. The Pennine Way, in particular, offers the experience of a wonderful range of different types of landscape. It skirts the moorland plateau in the Stainmore Gap, crosses the shallow valleys of Baldersdale and Lunedale, then drops into Teesdale. The riverside section along the Tees provides an intimate look at the river itself and at the waterfalls of High and Low Force and Cauldron Snout, the flower-rich meadows and walls of the valley floor, the dark cliffs of Holwick and Cronkley Scars and Falcon Clints, the juniper scrub, and the white-painted buildings.

The route passes the wide waters of Cow Green Reservoir before heading across the moorland ridge. After only a relatively short distance, the ground falls suddenly away to form the cliffs and graceful slopes of High Cup and, looking the full length of the absolutely symmetrical U-shaped valley, the Vale of Eden that can be glimpsed beyond. Dropping down the scarp, through bands of limestone crags, the complexities of the slate intrusions appear, with Dufton and Knock Pikes forming an impressive skyline. Dufton itself is a typical, red sandstone scarp-foot village, surrounded by the red soils and drumlin landscapes of the Vale of Eden. The national trail then climbs the scarp again, past the other side of Dufton Pike; passes along the moorland summits of Great Dun Fell and Cross Fell, through spectacular, wild moorland landscapes with extensive views if clear; then drops again through more moorland to South Tynedale at Garrigill. From here, there is wooded pastoral scenery along the dale to Alston and beyond, climbing briefly up to the moorland fringes to Whitley Castle, down to the dale bottom again, and finally up to the moors once more along the route of the Roman Maiden Way, before leaving the area altogether. Almost every type of characteristic landscape is encountered on this route.

*Dale head landscapes mark the transition from the sheltered dale to the open moorland, with settlement, enclosure and cultivation often at their highest limits.*

*The more pastoral character of the dales provides a welcome contrast to the open moorland.*

# 4. Perceptions of the North Pennines landscape

Literature, descriptive writings and art provide evidence about the way in which people have perceived the North Pennines landscape over time. Such material is generally only available for the past 200 years, from the late eighteenth century. Prior to that, the record of the area is more concerned with folklore than with landscape.

## Early accounts

Myths and legends abound. For example, King Arthur and his knights are supposed to lie asleep in caves at the Sneep on the River Derwent, and Allen-a-dale, one of Robin Hood's merry men, may have come from Allendale.

Early accounts of the character of the area are few. John Leland, the King's Antiquary, on his extensive travels through England (4), passed through Wolsingham, Frosterley, Stanhope, Eastgate and Westgate to St John's Chapel in Weardale. He comments on the Bishop of Durham's deer park "rudely enclosed with stone" and on the fertility of the dale itself, noting that "though the upper part of Weardale be not very fertile of corn, yet is there very fine grass in the dale itself where the river passeth". Defoe bypassed the area on his travels, but described the scarp viewed from a distance as a "wall of brass", perhaps because of the glowing colours of the grassland in low evening or winter sun.

## An area of aesthetic shadow

Even when writing about landscape, and landscape painting, became more common, from the picturesque period at the end of the eighteenth century, it must be said that, with the very notable exception of Teesdale, the North Pennines area is one of relative aesthetic shadow compared with the neighbouring uplands of the Lake District, the Yorkshire Dales and the Roman Wall area of Northumberland. This means that there are fewer associations with figures of national literary or artistic significance than in other similar parts of the country. This may be for a number of reasons, including remoteness and inaccessibility, lack of knowledge or underrating of the landscape, and the widespread impact of lead mining, which would have created industrial landscapes in many parts of the area by the end of the eighteenth century.

## The Rokeby connection and Turner in Teesdale

Some of the more significant artistic and literary associations are with the lower part of the Tees Valley, which, for a variety of reasons, was excluded from the AONB. The fame of this area centres on Rokeby Hall and Park, situated alongside the Tees outside Barnard Castle, and owned in the nineteenth century by the Morritt family. In 1805, John Sell Cotman stayed at Rokeby and, among other local subjects, painted the confluence of the Tees and the Greta. The work, *Greta Bridge*, is said to be one of the best known of all English watercolours. Sir Walter Scott made a number of visits to the Hall between 1802 and 1831, and in 1813 named his famous poem *Rokeby* after it. In the poem Scott mentions the village of Bowes, which lies on the very edge of the AONB. The popularity of the landscape around Barnard Castle grew with the publication of Scott's poem and, at least partly as a result of this, Teesdale itself became increasingly known for its scenery.

Teesdale has always been by far the most well-known landscape in the area. It was painted by Thomas Smith of Derby in 1751, by George Lambert in 1761, and then, more importantly, was visited by J.M.W. Turner, first in 1797, and then in 1816 on his tour of Yorkshire (5). In August 1816, he went to Greta Bridge, and sketched a number of scenes there, then sketched at Wycliffe Hall, Brignall and Egglestone. He moved on to Barnard Castle, made a detour to Bowes, where he sketched the village, church and Norman Castle keep, then followed the moorland road, which now forms part of the boundary to the AONB, across Deepdale to Cotherstone and on to Middleton-in-Teesdale, where he stayed. He made three sketches there, two of the town bridge and one of the bridge over the Tees.

Turner then headed west to the wilder reaches of Teesdale, following approximately the route of the modern Pennine Way. He stopped at Low Force, where he was particularly interested in the Wynch Bridge, which he sketched from the Holwick side, before proceeding to High Force. He spent some time there, and made several sketches both from above and below the falls.

Cauldron Snout was the next port of call, and there he sketched the full length of the falls in one view, although *Chain Bridge over the River Tees*, the finished work, bears little resemblance to reality or to his original sketch. Turner then crossed the high moorland summits, completing two brief sketches at High Cup, before retreating to the Inn at Dufton at the foot of the scarp. Some of the scenes sketched on this tour were turned, in 1817 and 1818, into completed watercolours for the *History of Richmondshire*, the first part of a *History of Yorkshire* for which Turner was commissioned by Longman and Co, the publishers.

After Turner's visit, Charles Dickens came to the area and found inspiration for *Nicholas Nickleby*, written in 1839. He stayed at Rokeby in 1832 and based the novel's Dotheboys Hall on a real institution at Bowes. Dickens wrote that when Nicholas Nickleby arrives in the area he "gazed upon the wild country round, covered with snow", referring no doubt to the North Pennine moors.

This distinguished group of early nineteenth century figures represent nationally important associations with Teesdale. Other important painters also drew inspiration from the area, including Dayes (1763-1804) and Hearne (1744-1806). John Martin

*Fall of the Tees*, c. 1825–26, J.M.W. Turner, (private collection, UK).

*Chain Bridge over the River Tees*, 1836, J.M.W. Turner, (private collection, UK).

*Cauldron Snout inspired one of Turner's paintings in the area.*

(1763-1854), the well-known painter of imaginary and fantastic sublime landscapes, came from Haydon Bridge. It has been suggested that "the wild scenery around Haydon Bridge, especially Allendale Gorge, has undoubtedly helped foster his lifelong fascination for the terrifying and spectacular" (6).

## Other landscape descriptions

Although not of the same national significance, there is a reasonable body of descriptive writing about the area, which throws light on the way in which various features of the landscape have been viewed over the years. It is, however, important to set these writings in their historical context.

A spate of mid- to late-nineteenth century Victorian 'picturesque' writing seems to have been inspired by the links with Scott, Turner and Dickens, and is focused on Teesdale, usually based on a very similar itinerary to that followed by Turner, and apparently much influenced by Scott's writing on the picturesque. The mid-nineteenth century taste for river valleys, and the turn of the century interest in windswept moorland, also had their effect. Victorian interests in science also meant that the flora of the area attracted attention in the nineteenth century, as did the social and economic history of lead mining.

The early part of the twentieth century brought few additions to the collection of writing, perhaps in part because of the advent of the camera, and also due to the effects of the First World War. In the 1930s, increasing mobility, and a growing tendency to visit the countryside for pleasure, brought a new series of writings in the form of guides and tour itineraries. Just before, and after, the Second World War, the birth of the access and national parks movement also had its effect, with increasing emphasis on the merits of wild, moorland scenery, and on long distance routes such as the Pennine Way.

More recently still, the attractions of the area for tourists have been emphasised in a series of tourist guides, and there have been growing efforts to attract more visitors to the area. As ecology and nature conservation have become major contemporary interests, the outstanding importance of the flora and fauna of the area has been a focus for comment, and there have also been more technical and policy statements relating to landscape protection.

In all of this material, a number of themes emerge relating to those aspects of the North Pennines landscape that have consistently attracted comment. They are summarised briefly below.

### Teesdale and the Whin Sill features

These are the most consistently described and admired parts of the landscape. Nineteenth century, and particulary Victorian writings, are filled with references to the variously picturesque, grand, romantic and sylvan scenery, based on guided excursions from the Wynch Bridge at Low Force, to High Force and sometimes beyond to Cauldron Snout. Richard Garland, describing his tour in 1804 (7), writes lyrically of the "strikingly bold and broken" scenery, the "carpets of gay flowers", the "boldness and irregularity" of the "majestic cliffs" of Cronkley Scar, and the "awe-striking beauty of the temple" of High Force. Adjectives used by writers at this time to describe the various falls include foaming, shaking, deafening, stunning, awful and sublime. The specialist interests in the area were apparently already well known. Two anonymous women, making the tour in 1877, stated the view that:

> "Teesdale may vie with any part of the kingdom; it is immortalised by poet and painter; the geologist and antiquarian find a wide field for research, while the botanist hails upper Teesdale as one of his richest fields of wealth."

The mid-nineteenth century also saw the publication of *Poems and Songs of Teesdale* (8) by Richard Watson, the Teesdale poet. Born in 1833, Watson was the son of a miner employed by the London Lead Company. His poems have been likened to those of Burns and were well received by both the press and the public. His great affection for the Teesdale landscape is a common thread in many of his poems, including *Lovely sweet vale of the Tees, My journey to work* and *Green Banks of the Tees*, in which he writes:

> "The sun is sinking, Mary,
> O'er the distant, western fells,
> and the birds have gone to rest love
> In the groves and hazel dells.
> Come and walk with me, my Mary,
> In the cool and evening breeze,
> Where the sweet wild flowers are blooming
> on the green banks of the Tees."

Similar sentiments, although perhaps less romantic than the Victorian ones in expression, occur throughout all of the descriptions, including the most contemporary. In 1969, Redfern (9), describes upper Teesdale in Autumn as "a feast of colour, backed by cloud dappled russet moors" and the white farms as like "daisies on a lawn". Wainwright, writing about the Pennine Way in 1985, suggests that the middle part of Teesdale should be savoured slowly because "nothing more scenically beautiful than this part of the valley will be met during the rest of the Way" (10). He enthuses about the river scenery, the flowers, the cascades and waterfalls and calls it "a walk of near perfection". To him, High Force is "The Tees' finest moment" and Cauldron Snout "the Tees in angry mood". Perhaps the last word should go to David Bellamy and Brendan Quayle, in their 1989 book *England's Last Wilderness* (11), who extol the virtues of the unique flora:

> "But above, below and all around are Teesdale's flowers. Delicate blue gentians, and pink primroses head a whole flowering of alpine and arctic plants which brighten each new spring.... Teesdale above all the dales is the jewel in the botanical crown of the North Pennines, a floral tribute from the past."

## High moorland landscapes

The influences of the picturesque period meant that early nineteenth century writers were not overly impressed by moorland landscapes, finding them bereft of the essential picturesque elements of trees and woodlands. So Garland, in 1804, finds that, above Cauldron Snout, "not a house, a tree or enclosure of any kind, interrupts the boundless waste; not one dash of cheerful green animates the black and dreary heath"(7).

Writing later in the century continues to be in a similar vein, but in 1890 William Wallace (3), while still arguing for the benefits to be gained by planting trees, refers to "scenes of grandeur and sublimity" which can be seen from the "tops of the mountains at the head of the Tyne, the Wear and the Tees." Shortly afterwards Boyle, writing in a publication of Walter Scott Ltd, suggests that:

> "There is scarcely a lonelier tract anywhere in England than the expanse of wild moor that fills up the whole area between Alston, Langdon Bridge and Dufton"(12).

A degree of ambivalence about moorland continues to appear, and in 1901, Bulmer (13) in a much-quoted statement, noted that "healthy moorland" distinguishes the Alston Moor parish, in spite of the fact that "over a wide extent the traveller searches in vain for a single spot of beauty on which to feast his weary eyes." In *Picturesque Weardale* (14), Egglestone describes the charms of the eastern moorland ridges above Stanhope, referring to the charming bloom of the heather and to the colour contrasts with bracken.

Since the 1930s, the growing interest in wild areas, and the growth of the access to moorland movement, have resulted in growing emphasis on the merits of moorland scenery. The attractions of remoteness, wilderness and arduous terrain are becoming increasingly appreciated. Douglas Ramsden summed up this view in 1947 when he wrote:

> "It is not everybody's country, but the taste may be acquired, and once formed it remains a possession of value. The North Pennine moors represent the ultimates in landscape. They are bare and empty regions which the sun quickens into a pale, subdued colouring. There are no trees and few flowers. The minutiae of details which distract the eyes in the woods and lanes of the valleys become less significant, and in their place is a new aspect of space"(15).

How true those statements are, even today, summing up as they do the divisions of opinion which still exist between those for whom wild upland moors are the epitome of fine landscape, and those who prefer the less hostile, more conventionally picturesque landscapes of dales and woodlands. Ramsden goes on to summarise the special qualities of the moorland, referring to the harmonious arrangement of masses, the bare outlines, the restful effect on the mind and, at the same time, the exhilaration derived from the sense of space and emptiness.

The summit ridge of Cross Fell and its companions is frequently described, with particular emphasis on the extent of views. Redfern describes the summit as "an arctic terrain which many lowlanders would barely believe existed in this country, let alone in England" and recalls an unforgettable experience standing on a moonlit January night on the "wilderness atop Cross Fell"(9). Wainwright describes the magnificent panorama viewed from the top when visibility is good, taking in all of the northern counties of England and beyond to the Solway Firth.

## Severe weather

There can be few areas in Britain where the severity of the weather is such a prominent feature of landscape descriptions. Sopwith, in 1833, refers to the rainy weather which "shrouds it with a very cheerless and uncomfortable aspect"(16). Many writers refer to the severe conditions that prevail on the summits, with Mitchell in 1979 suggesting that for about 280 days a year Cross Fell wears "a bonnet of cloud or a shroud of mist"(17). He also talks of the need to "take a spade to bed in winter"(18). John Pennington (19) describes the beauties of the winter landscape, especially the snow piled up against the walls, and in Hannah Hauxwell's story *Seasons of my life*, Barry Cockcroft notes that when snow lightly dusts the urban areas "you can be sure that Baldersdale and the rest of the High Pennines will be thigh deep"(20).

The Helm wind, which is a special feature of Cross Fell, the scarp and the Vale of Eden, receives special mention in many descriptions. It has been reported to achieve many legendary effects such as lifting slates, scattering hay, blowing the beaks off geese, and stopping rooks in mid-flight so that they have to walk back to their nests! Boyle describes in some detail the peculiar cloud formations and light effects associated with the wind (12).

## The scarp and the Vale of Eden

Defoe's early reference to the 'wall of brass' is mirrored elsewhere. Ramsden (15) describes the view towards the scarp for the traveller by road or rail through Appleby to Carlisle as "probably the most impressive" of the Pennines. He describes how, in summer, "the sun reveals starkly all the details of the weathered slopes and draws out the subdued colouring of scar and grassy edge". The pikes of Dufton and Knock attract comment, with Boyle describing a sunset as giving Dufton Pike "the appearance of a burning mountain." The view over the Vale of Eden evokes superlatives. Wainwright (10) considers it "the fairest panorama yet seen" on the Pennine Way. He also refers to the contrast between the "stark, upland wilderness" of the moors above, and the "quiet, comforting beauty" of the Vale below, with the "inspiring sight" of the Lakeland fells beyond. In 1947, Ramsden caught the essence of the sudden changes of atmosphere and light that are often seen from the scarp and can transform the landscape:

"The scene was still grey and the vast, lighter-coloured plain seemed to bound the dark outlines of the fells, like a sea beyond the line of sentinel pikes. Then gradually the clouds lifted clear above the Lakeland pikes and the sun shone through, bringing out detail and colour, and lifting melancholy from the spirit."

The Whin Sill feature of High Cup receives notable attention from many awe-struck writers. Garland, in 1804, describes it as a "huge chasm" which opens "to a wide and delightful country"(7). Ramsden notes the dark cliffs, green slope, lines and fans of scree and "a tiny stream which seemed lost in the vast basin of the gorge". Wainwright describes the sudden revelation of the gorge after crossing the moors as "awesome", and the feature itself as a "profound abyss.... a geological phenomenon, a natural wonder."

## Other dales

It must be said that by comparison with Teesdale, the other dales have received much less attention from descriptive writers. These dales may have suffered from the impact of lead mining and were therefore less 'scenic' in the nineteenth century. Other dales also lacked the special connection with the likes of Turner, Scott and Dickens that Teesdale had. Recent guides and books, notably *England's Last Wilderness*, which describes the area dale by dale, have tried to rectify the imbalance. Prior to that, the main sources are writers who were primarily interested in lead mining, although one Victorian picturesque book *The Tyne and its Tributaries* (21), extols the virtues of the northern dales. Here it is noted that in South Tynedale "visitors are rarely seen." It describes Garrigill as a pretty place with "its bright little green surrounded by white-washed cottages and many trees, making sweet contrast to the dark hills among which it is set." This is a view shared by Wainwright, who considers the village an "oasis of greenery" after the bleak moors. However, he also finds that "though South Tynedale is attractive, nowhere is there the charm and excitement of Teesdale."

Redfern, in 1969, wrote that the head of South Tynedale is "reminiscent of the Southern Uplands of Scotland", while Brian Spencer, in 1986, thought that the character of the northern dales was quite different from Teesdale and Weardale, describing them as "Northumbrian geographically and politically" (22). Weardale has not produced as many descriptions as Teesdale, and most have concentrated on its status as 'the lead dale'. Brian Spencer, for example notes that:

"The spread of hamlets and small holdings in Upper Weardale is typical of the way mining communities developed at the height of the mining industry. The way the dozens of paths, like parts of a spider's web, wander across the hillsides tell us of an area linked to a single purpose."

The promising title *Picturesque Weardale* (14), produced in 1916, is a collection of black and white photographs of the dale, but few illustrate the wider landscape beyond the towns and villages.

In writing about East and West Allendale, Palmer refers to the "beautiful vale of Whitfield" and to the views in the area over the wooded Allen gorges. He also describes the "sublime masses of countless tree forms" within the woods, and the picturesque character of the river in the gorge. He suggests that the painter John Martin may have found inspiration there. Only scant reference is made to the higher parts of the dales. Palmer refers to "a district of bleak fells and moorlands called Allenheads" where, "wild as the region is considered to be, Mr. Beaumont's park.... is famous for its beauty". A more recent guide describes Allenheads as a genuinely picturesque village lying in a tree-lined hollow.

In all of these dales where lead mining has been so influential, there are many comments on the changes brought by the rise and fall of the industry. John Hodgson, in his *History of Northumberland* (6) writes:

> "The little Valley of the Nent was once a fairy land, and had its flowery meadows, and wild shaws and bosky breays, and Nentsbury for its capital, till the wealth of mining speculations began to improve and enlarge the narrow stripe of enclosed land that fringed the margins of its chrystal stream; and blotch its gemmed and emerald fields with the rubbish of its mines and levels, and gutter its head and sides and poison its sweet waters...."

Mitchell (17) recounts how in 1860, an old lady remembered the time when not a tree stood between Alston and Nenthead and compares this with the tree-planting carried out by the mining companies.

Derwentdale is mentioned relatively little, although when it is, there is considerable emphasis on the charms of Blanchland and its history, and on the wooded gorges of Horsleyhope ravine and the Sneep. George Bellam wrote:

> "The visitor has before him a view that may fearlessly be compared with the best that England can produce. Down below him is the conjunction of the precipitous wooded ravine of the Horsley Hope, the Hysehope and the Sneep, cutting far back into the heather-covered hill. No pencil can convey an adequate impression of the scene"(23).

## Contemporary perceptions

Most contemporary descriptions of the North Pennines can be found in tourist guides or in 'official' policy statements about the area. The guides tend to give detailed itineraries and information on local history, relying largely on photographs to evoke the qualities of the landscape. In a recent guidebook, *Weardale, Allendale and South Tynedale* (24), J. Keith Proud introduces the area by saying that "this magnificent part of rural England possesses some of the wildest, and bleakest unspoilt, natural landscapes in Britain" and goes on to refer to the lead dales as "a very beautiful region of Britain, as yet relatively undiscovered."

In the title of the only comprehensive book on the landscape, history and culture of the area, David Bellamy and Brendan Quayle have coined the phrase "England's Last Wilderness". They note the unique qualities that set it apart from other areas, and emphasise the importance of the flora and fauna in this uniqueness:

> "That magic of the North Pennines, their plants, animals and birds, sets the area apart from the other great upland landscapes of England and Wales. It is different in other respects too. The landforms may not be as rugged and spectacular as those of the Lake District to the west, and the Yorkshire Dales to the south, but the bleak rolling moors, sweeping down into lush green valleys, together with the rich heritage of the lead mining era, and some remarkable landforms like High Cup Nick and High Force, make it special – uniquely Pennine."

Official statements appeared in profusion at the time of the public inquiry into the designation of the area as an area of outstanding natural beauty. The view of the Countryside Commission was summarised by the inspector as follows:

> "The North Pennines possessed unique qualities and there was no other area, even in national parks, where these qualities were so apparent. It was impressive, majestic, wild, high, and unfriendly. The landscape features of both high moor and dale, which together created the typical Pennines scene, were, judged against the standard of other designated areas in England and Wales, including national parks, of outstanding quality"(25).

Many others supported this general view. Even those who opposed the designation were generally in agreement about the beauty of the area, but were prepared to argue about how natural or outstanding it was, and whether designation was the best way to protect its qualities.

What, though, of the views of ordinary people who live in or visit the area? Unfortunately, there is little evidence about this. One survey in Lunedale parish in 1979 (26) asked local farmers about their favourite places and their attitudes to the landscape. Teesdale, with its river, trees and waterfalls, was named several times. Others mentioned the remoteness of the moors and the views afforded by the treeless landscape, the lack of industry and the 'unmanaged but tidy' appearance of much of the countryside. Some felt that because they had lived in the area all of their lives they could not identify what it was that was special about it. This clearly illustrates how different groups of people, and different individuals, may attach varying value to what they see in a landscape.

# 5. Forces for change

It will already be clear from this report that evolving patterns of land use have played a major part in shaping the landscape over the centuries. This continues to be the case today, and hill and upland farming, grouse-moor management, forestry, mining, quarrying and the associated needs of settlement, transport and communication, can all influence the future of the North Pennines. Change is, of course, an essential part of every landscape, and designation as an AONB is not intended to freeze the North Pennines at a particular point in time. Rather, the aim is to strike a balance between essential development and conservation of the features that cause the landscape to be highly valued.

There has been no overall assessment of recent change in the area. The 1979 study of Lunedale parish, carried out as part of the Countryside Commission's *Upland Landscapes Study* (26) examined change in this extensive part of the area in some detail, although the picture may well have changed in the twelve years since then. More recent evidence relating to pressures for change also featured in the public examination of the AONB proposals.

It appears that there are numerous small-scale changes taking place in the landscape. None, perhaps, compare in scale or extent with the changes which took place in the eighteenth and nineteenth centuries, with the rise and fall of the mining industry, and the construction of the stone field enclosures. However, the situation is finely balanced, and the landscape is influenced by a wide range of forces for change which could, under certain circumstances, produce widespread, potentially dramatic, and often undesirable change in the future.

## Changes in farming

Hill and upland farming is largely responsible for creating and maintaining the characteristic landscape of the moorland and, in particular, of the dales. Since the war, hill farming has been heavily dependent upon government support systems. These have generally encouraged more intensive production and greater specialisation, which has had consequences for the landscape. Changes that have taken place since the 1940s include: improvement of meadows and pastures by fertilising, or sometimes drainage and seeding; changes in management, such as substitution of silage-making for traditional hay-making; introduction of modern farm buildings, and replacement of walls with fences. These changes have had greatest impact in the dales, where the most significant threats have been to the traditional flower-rich hay meadows that are such a feature of the landscape, especially in Teesdale and Weardale.

The character of the moorland landscapes depends both on grazing by sheep and on traditional burning of grouse moors. The extent of moorland appears to have remained relatively constant in recent years, although there have been changes at the margins, above the dales. Here, some pasture has been allowed to revert to moorland, and some moorland has been reclaimed as grass land.

The fine grain of the moorland landscape depends on the colours and textures of moorland vegetation, and on patterns, including those which result from burning and other forms of management. The nature of the vegetation depends on levels of sheep grazing. Numbers of sheep have almost certainly increased significantly, and the resultant heavy grazing has encouraged an increase in grass moorland at the expense of heather, with consequences for wildlife interest as well as landscape, and has contributed to peat erosion, and created higher demand for fencing on the moors. The picture is, of course, complex and the farming community would not necessarily agree that over-stocking is a problem. Nevertheless, some grouse moor owners are actively buying back grazing rights, in order to reduce stocking levels, and this is indicative of their concern.

Other changes that are influencing the moorland landscape are the spread of bracken as a result of changes in management, an increase in bare peat as a result of erosion, and the use of moorland 'gripping' which involves the cutting of straight, parallel lines of open drains across the moorland. This introduces a regular, geometrical pattern to the otherwise irregular patterns of landform and vegetation.

At the same time, it is becoming increasingly difficult for hill farms to provide a satisfactory living in such a marginal area. Farmers are therefore leaving the land, and farms are being amalgamated. There is pressure for those who remain to intensify further. At the same time, many of the characteristic features of the landscape, which rely on traditional patterns of farming to maintain them, are decaying. Walls are collapsing, barns and some farmsteads falling derelict, trees dying and not being replaced, woodlands being grazed out and bracken encroaching on moorland. The changes are not yet dramatic, although they are very apparent to those familiar with the area. However, given the economic pressures on farming, and the likelihood of changes in the Common Agricultural Policy both to reduce surpluses and to cut subsidies, this situation could change very rapidly, bringing the prospect of widespread decay and dereliction in the landscape. Although potentially detrimental to the existing character of the landscape, some people might argue that in the longer term such changes could open the way to creating new forms of 'wilderness' landscape for the future.

To ensure that such changes, to both dale and moor, do not undermine the special qualities of the landscape and the outstanding nature conservation value of the area, there needs to be more emphasis on support for farming management practices that

*The future of the North Pennines landscape depends on the survival of environmentally sensitive upland farming.*

*If upland farming were to decline, remote farms such as this could be abandoned and traditional landscape features fall into decay.*

are in harmony with the landscape, while also helping to keep farmers on the land, and so contribute to maintaining the upland farming community. Some steps have already been taken in this direction by the inclusion of Teesdale, Weardale and Rookhope in the Pennine Dales Environmentally Sensitive Area (ESA). The ESA mechanism allows the Ministry of Agriculture to make payments to farmers to encourage them to continue traditional management of hay meadows, to maintain the rough allotment grazings, and to maintain characteristic landscape features such as walls and traditional buildings. Although the scheme is voluntary, the response has been good, and the financial incentives that are available should play a vital part in maintaining the traditional character of the landscape of these dales. It is hoped that a similar scheme may in future be introduced for the whole of the North Pennines area.

## Woodlands and forests

Although not great in area, woodlands and forests make a very important contribution to the landscape. Over the years, there have been concerns that afforestation will become a major force for change in the landscape. However, the AONB currently remains surprisingly free of the large-scale coniferous plantations which are present in so many other upland areas of Britain. There are a number of factors contributing to this including: the significant area of common land; the attitudes of the large estates, who have not generally considered forestry to be a desirable alternative to sheep farming and grouse moors; and the physical limitations on commercial timber crops over much of the high moorland, due to high altitude, exposure and poor peaty soils.

There appears to be little prospect of significant afforestation taking place in the short term. Changes in financial incentives relating to forestry, and a ministerial statement to the effect that there will be no more extensive conifer planting in the English uplands, have both contributed to this, as has the continuing importance of grouse shooting and common land. However, circumstances could change again in the longer term, and pressures for forestry planting could increase. The plantations that do occur in the area, both large and small, demonstrate clearly what the impact could be. They often have regular, geometric shapes and straight boundaries that stand out in the landscape. These plantations do, however, date from a period before the forestry industry became aware of the need to take full account of environmental considerations and to design plantations to fit more naturally within the landscape. The same mistakes would almost certainly not be repeated today.

## Opportunities for new planting

It is therefore important to recognise the way in which new forestry and woodland planting can make a positive contribution to the landscape. A recent forestry capability survey of the area has given some clues to assist with this. It shows that large parts of the high moorlands are generally incapable of growing timber crops, and that the land with greatest flexibility for growing a variety of timber crops with good yields is in the dale bottoms. This land, however, is unlikely to be available for planting because it supports the in-bye meadows and pastures that play such a crucial part in the farming system.

The flexibility of the land to support a range of timber-producing trees decreases with altitude, and is variously affected by exposure, climate, nutrients available in the soil, steepness of slope or wetness of soil. Although forestry economics generally favour coniferous species, there is little doubt that from a landscape point of view, deciduous and mixed woods are to be preferred. Such planting is only likely to be possible on the more flexible types of land that are generally found lower down the dale sides, and in the eastern parts of the area where the land is lower-lying.

The landscape types that are generally wholly unsuited to new planting are the scarp slope, except on the very lowest foot slopes, and in valleys such as Geltsdale, the high moorland summits, and the moorland ridges. The moorland plateau in the Stainmore depression has been identified on a number of occasions as a moorland area that could accept substantial new planting, because of its bleak and featureless character. Many would disagree with this, considering the wilderness character of this area to be important in its own right. Proximity of this area to the A66 and to the Pennine Way also means that any such proposal would be very sensitive.

There are some situations in the dales where modest planting may be acceptable, if it is carefully conceived and well designed, taking full regard of landscape and other environmental considerations. It is particularly important that the scale, shape and form of new plantations should be appropriate to the natural form and flow of the land, with special attention being given to the nature of woodland edges. The balance between open and wooded ground is also important, as is the use of appropriate species in carefully considered mixes that favour deciduous and mixed woodlands.

In Teesdale, the particular character and important features of the landscape make it unlikely that any significant planting would be acceptable. In Weardale, there may be limited opportunities on the middle dale slopes and on the dale head, where a judicious mixture of well-designed felling and carefully planned new planting could bring about improvements in the existing, far from sympathetic, plantations. There may also be some scope for limited, small-scale and sympathetic planting in the north–south dales and in Derwentdale. Well-designed broadleaved or mixed planting may be possible on the middle or lower dale slopes and, if well-designed, could make a positive contribution to the landscape. Land in the middle range of forestry capability classes, especially where slope is the limiting factor, appears likely to be particularly well-suited to such planting, where other constraints allow. Such land often supports the existing woodland in the dales.

There may also be scope for planting in the upland fringes, although agricultural value may prevent this in some parts. The limestone fringes are not suited to planting, but opportunities may be found in the fringe areas on the northern and eastern margins.

## Existing woodlands

It is not only new planting that can bring change in the landscape. Changes to existing woodlands can also be significant. In the past some of the steep, deciduous gorge woodlands in lower Allendale and lower Derwentdale have been partly replanted with conifers, changing their contribution to the landscape and reducing their wildlife value. Changes in emphasis in forestry now mean that such changes are less likely to continue in the future. Other broadleaved woodlands are suffering from lack of management and from grazing by stock, which prevents the trees from regenerating naturally. The woodlands that line the ghylls flowing down the dale sides are particularly vulnerable to the effects of grazing, as few are enclosed to keep stock out. If this situation is not rectified, these important landscape features may gradually disappear. Positive management is essential to ensure that woodlands continue to play their part in the landscape. The introduction of some form of financial incentive or grant support is likely to be the best way of achieving this.

## Mineral working

It needs only a cursory glance at old photographs of the lead dales, at the height of the lead mining boom, to realise just how much the landscape changed with the decline of the industry. There have been periods of abandonment, neglect and destruction, and many mining remains have been damaged or lost. However, the importance of these remains is now being increasingly recognised and a number are being conserved, restored and opened to the public.

Mining and quarrying is recognised as a long-standing land use in the area, and the heritage of historic mining now has its own value. However, the scale and nature of modern operations is often very different from the old methods, and can have a major and detrimental effect on the landscape. There are significant mineral reserves in the area, including limestone, sandstone, ganister, coal, sand and gravel, igneous rock, fluorspar and barytes. Mining and quarrying will therefore continue to play a part in the area and will help to maintain local employment. However, because of the importance and sensitivity of the landscape, new schemes and extensions of current workings will need to be scrutinised very carefully. A balance must be found between environmental, social and economic interests, with particular attention being given to the type of landscape within which the proposal is located, its effect on landscape character, its visibility and other aspects of siting and design. Schemes of a scale and nature appropriate to their surroundings will be more readily accommodated than others. Proposals for stone quarrying and open-cast coal mining may both have a particular influence on the area in future, and will need to be assessed very carefully. Open cast mining in particular is unlikely to be acceptable in the AONB.

## New development

Most new development is likely to be located in villages and towns lying outside the area, although there will always be a need for some new building in the AONB. Such development, although small in scale, can have a cumulative effect on the landscape if proper attention is not given to careful siting and good design. The greatest need is for new buildings to be carefully sited, to reflect local vernacular styles, and to use typical local materials. There are some good examples in and around the area of what can be achieved by good design and use of local stone, in housing, tourist developments and engineering works such as bridge improvements. There are also examples to show how bad the results can be when such care is not taken, including some glaring evidence of the use of red brick in what is essentially a stone environment.

With so many abandoned farmsteads and farm buildings in the area, it is not surprising that many are being purchased and restored, either as holiday homes for let, as second homes, as commuter residences or as retirement homes. The effects of this are as much to do with changes in the social structure of local communities as with physical consequences for the landscape. Of course, these conversions have a positive effect, in that they ensure that these buildings remain in the landscape and do not fall into dereliction. However, the changes that result can also introduce a degree of 'gentrification' into a very simple style of vernacular building. While the cumulative effects are subtle, this could still bring change to the landscape on a small scale.

Tourism is being actively promoted as a new source of economic employment and activity for the area. This may bring its own requirements for conversions and new buildings. Schemes should be small-scale and sympathetic to their surroundings, drawing on both local culture and environment. Development pursued along these lines is unlikely to bring any significant change to the area, although increases in the number of visitors will in itself change the empty, undiscovered character of much of the landscape. There may also be further attempts to introduce large-scale tourist developments – perhaps holiday villages, major recreation facilities or other attractions. These can have a very significant impact, because they are often completely out of character with the landscape – being imposed upon it rather than drawing inspiration from it. Such development is generally inappropriate in special areas such as the North Pennines.

The high altitude and exposed nature of the area bring other special pressures for development. Communication masts have been located on the summit ridge, and a long-range radar station for the Civil Aviation Authority has been built on Great Dun Fell, replacing the older buildings on the same site and benefiting from the height of the moorland ridge at this point. Proposals have also been made to locate a trial wind-powered electricity generating station on Langdon Common, although these have currently been shelved. Such proposals clearly introduce completely new and alien features into the landscape – masts, the white 'radome' on Great Dun Fell and a modern windfarm. They bring significant change to the 'wilderness' character of the high moorland summits, reducing the sense of apparent naturalness and freedom from human influence. Such structures provoke a mixture of responses. Many people certainly find them an alien intrusion in open landscapes, whilst others consider them to be fine, almost sculptural features. Clearly, they are controversial and, in general, it is to be hoped that further man-made additions to the wild moorland landscapes of the North Pennines AONB can be avoided in future.

Overall, the picture appears to be one of a landscape whose future is finely balanced, with scope for significant change if the prospects for different upland land uses, and especially hill farming, should alter. The character and quality of the landscape can be maintained, given the support of the many individuals, authorities and agencies who are involved. Appropriate forms of support for environmentally sensitive farming and essential woodland management are urgently needed; practical countryside management projects will continue to have an important role to play, and clear, appropriate planning policies and sensitive development control are needed. All of these mechanisms need to be geared to protecting the particular qualities that make the North Pennines landscape so important.

# 6. The importance of the North Pennines landscape

*Much of the special identity of the North Pennines is based on the simplicity, extent and wildness of the moors and the intricate, enclosed and complex character of the dales.*

It is rare for the special qualities of a landscape to have been so thoroughly examined as has been the case in the North Pennines. The public inquiry established a precedent in ruling that landscape quality can be assessed on the basis of "the consensus of informed opinion, allied with the 'trained eye', and commonsense". The inquiry also made it clear that 'natural beauty' includes consideration of flora, fauna, geological and physiographical features, and does not exclude landscapes that are the product of human activities over the centuries. Designation as an AONB simply recognises that as a society we attach special national importance to a certain landscape. The reasons for this can be many and varied. They are summarised below with specific reference to the North Pennines landscape.

## A distinct type of landscape

The North Pennines form a distinct geological landscape unit. Although the area has much in common with other parts of the Pennines, it is distinguished by the particular combination of limestone features, with a major ore field, and with spectacular intrusions of the Whin Sill. Geologically, therefore, it combines features characteristic of the Yorkshire Dales to the south with others more typical of the Northumberland National Park to the north. This unusual geology, linked with the great height and exposure of the moorland summits, creates a special type of landscape which is unique in England.

## Wilderness qualities

The North Pennines have been labelled 'England's Last Wilderness', and there is little doubt that the area lives up to this name. The moorland landscapes provide an experience that is typified by unbroken extent, relative remoteness, high altitude, a severe climate, sometimes difficult terrain and apparent, if not actual, naturalness. These characteristics combine to create an illusion of wilderness that is highly valued by growing numbers of people. The moorland summit ridge of the North Pennines is unique in England in being of sufficient extent to provide this sort of experience, and only the remote parts of Wales and Scotland can vie with it for the necessary qualities. The moorland plateau and, to a lesser extent, the moorland ridges, have similar characteristics. The wilderness qualities of the area will become increasingly important as nearby areas such as the national parks of the Lake District and the Yorkshire Dales become ever more crowded.

## Aesthetic qualities of the landscape

The North Pennines share many of the aesthetic qualities of other areas of designated upland landscape in England and Wales but, taken as a whole, the AONB also has its own strong identity and sense of place. This identity is based on the unique geology and the particular pattern of man's activities in the area over the centuries, and is most evident in the rich contrasts between moorland and dales. This creates great diversity, as well as the typical unfolding sequence of landscapes that is revealed when travelling through the area. This sense of place is highlighted by the dramatic landscape features which accompany the intrusions of the Whin Sill, notably the waterfalls of High and Low Force and Cauldron Snout, the cliff scars in Teesdale, and the spectacular valley of High Cup, as well as by other individual features such as the Allen and Derwent gorges.

The important contrasts depend upon the individual qualities of the different types of landscape. The moorland landscapes are valued for their long views, uninterrupted extent, uniformity and simplicity of landform, with horizontal sweeps, interlocking ridges and smooth lines. Together these create an exhilarating sense of space and freedom. These landscapes are enlivened by the varying colours and textures of moorland vegetation, by the many patterns on the land, and by the characteristic sights and sounds of upland birds.

The dales are valued for their more enclosed, sheltered and domestic landscapes. They are diverse and complex, with striking patterns and textures in the walled meadows and pastures. Simple vernacular buildings, including farmsteads, barns and villages, built in local stone, add to the harmony and unity of the landscape. The river corridors have their own small-scale landscape with waterfalls, rapids and riffles and steep, wooded valley sides. These are frequently the most picturesque parts of the dales.

The edges of the upland area vary widely, but the western scarp, together with the Vale of Eden at its foot, has outstanding qualities. With dramatic and varied landforms, panoramic views, unusual effects of light and weather, and the gems of the red sandstone villages at the scarp foot, this is one of the most attractive parts of the North Pennines.

Every part of the North Pennines has its own particular character and qualities, but some areas are particularly notable. They include Teesdale itself, perhaps the most well-loved part of the whole area, the high moorland summits, the southern scarp and the wooded gorges of lower Allendale and lower Derwentdale. These areas have perhaps the finest combinations of the characteristic features and special aesthetic qualities that are typical of the North Pennine landscapes, and they have also been most consistently described and admired by writers and artists over the past 200 years.

## An historic mining landscape

The rise and fall of the lead mining industry in Britain has left indelible marks on the landscape, not only in the physical remnants of mining and related activity, but also in the pattern of settlement and farming associated with it. The whole of the North Pennines is therefore of value as a historic mining landscape, with Weardale, Rookhope, the Nent Valley, South Tynedale, West Allendale and Allendale in particular providing notable examples of the physical evidence that remains. Although mining may have had adverse consequences for the landscape when the industry was at its height, the 'lead landscapes' that now remain have considerable value in their own right, even if they are not always the most scenically attractive parts of the AONB.

## Specialist interests in the landscape

Even if the landscape were not considered to be of outstanding value, the North Pennines would still be considered to be nationally, and indeed internationally, important because of its unique flora and fauna. There are a number of habitats and combinations of species that occur only in this area, as well as an exceptionally rich collection of rare species. There are also important examples of more widely distributed habitats and an important range of bird species. In recognition of their importance, large areas are either National Nature Reserves (NNRs) or designated Sites of Special Scientific Interest (SSSIs), and the Moorhouse area is a Biosphere Reserve.

The geology and geomorphology of the area is also of great value, with a wide range of notable characteristics. These include Whin Sill, ore field, limestone and glacial and periglacial features, some of which are also recognised by designation as SSSIs.

The archaeological and historical value of the area is also high. As well as the lead mining remains, there is important evidence from many different periods of history, including old field systems and settlement sites, Roman remains, castles and fortified buildings, churches and larger houses. There are large numbers of listed buildings, conservation areas and archaeological sites.

Although these specialist interests have their own importance, they also contribute greatly to the landscape character of the North Pennines. The flora and fauna, the geological and geomorphological features, and the archaeological and historical sites are all an inseparable part of what makes the landscape so special. Recognition and understanding of these features adds greatly to enjoyment of the landscape, although even without this understanding their contribution is clear for all to see.

## Recognition of the qualities of the landscape

The North Pennines landscape has never been as fashionable as places such as the Lake District and the Yorkshire Dales. With the exception of Teesdale, and a few other beauty spots, the area has not been as well known or as frequently visited as other areas, and this situation has continued up until the present, with the area still not as firmly established on the tourist map as its upland neighbours. This appears to be due to its remoteness and to the lack of a fashionable association with the great tours of earlier centuries, to the historic effects of mining, and to a lack of knowledge of the area's qualities. It is a landscape which has been the province of the connoisseur, of the seeker of unknown places, and of those who relish a departure from the well-worn routes. This relative lack of popularity does not mean that people do not like the landscape, but simply that many do not know about it. However, this is changing, as more publicity is given to the special qualities of the area and to its quiet, undiscovered character.

Those in the know have always recognised how much the landscape has to offer. The eighteenth and nineteenth century artists who painted in the area, including Turner and perhaps Martin, the many writers who have described its charms, and the lovers of wild places drawn to the moors, have all been inspired by its many delights. These people represent the beginnings of a consensus of informed opinion of the view that this is indeed a landscape of high quality. This consensus was officially recognised after the Second World War, firstly by the inclusion in the 1945 Dower Report of the North Pennines as a reserve area for designation as a national park, and then by inclusion in the 1947 Hobhouse report as a proposed conservation area. The list of conservation areas in this report provided the basis for the subsequent designation of AONBs. In 1951, the routing through the area of the Pennine Way, the first long distance footpath in England and Wales, helped to confirm its value, and in the 1950s all of the county councils identified the North Pennines as an area of great landscape value in their development plans.

In 1973, the Countryside Commission announced their intention to seek designation of the area as an AONB. In 1974, a working party of members of various voluntary and amenity groups produced a report on the landscape character of an area generally referred to as the North Pennines, and recommended that it should be designated as a national park or, if this proved impossible, as an AONB. In the same year, Cumbria County Council proposed designation of the North Pennines in Cumbria as an AONB, and the other counties also supported this general proposal. The official consensus about the value of the landscape was therefore established.

Despite lengthy arguments at the public inquiry, few people suggested that the area was not beautiful. Some argued that certain parts were not as beautiful as others, and some that the North Pennines was not of the same landscape quality as other upland areas. In the end, the inspector and his fellow assessors drew their own conclusions, by formalising the consensus and confirming that the area was of such outstanding quality as to merit designation.

## Prospects for change

The North Pennines landscape is undoubtedly very special. Key features which contribute particularly to its overall character and quality are: semi-natural moorland and grassland vegetation; deciduous woodlands; the matrix of stone walls in the dales; unimproved flower-rich meadows and pastures; vernacular stone buildings; remains of the lead mining industry; geomorphological features; and river corridor landscapes.

The future of the landscape is finely balanced, and there are a number of forces that may lead to change in the characteristics of the landscape in the future. Detrimental effects on the landscape could result from:

- further improvement of meadows and pastures;

- removal, abandonment or lack of maintenance of stone walls;

- large-scale, poorly located or inappropriately designed forestry or woodland planting;

- loss of, or decline in, the value of deciduous woodlands;

- reclamation or improvement of moorland vegetation, or large-scale introduction of moorland gripping;

- changes in vegetation patterns, particularly loss of heather due to increased stocking levels;

- destruction of, or damage to, lead mining remains;

- inappropriate large-scale development;

- introduction of man-made structures on the moorlands;

- unsympathetic small-scale development and building conversion;

- inappropriate tourism initiatives.

Mechanisms exist to ensure that if these forces for change do become more significant, they can be controlled. There is, however, a need for partnership between all those with an interest in the area, to ensure that the right balance is struck between the need to conserve the landscape and the need to maintain local communities and meet their social and economic needs. New forms of economic support may be necessary to help to achieve this.

## A nationally important landscape

To summarise, the North Pennines are valued as a unique landscape unit with a distinctive geology and an unusually large extent of high, exposed semi-natural moorland which has outstanding wilderness qualities. The landscape is characterised by dramatic contrasts and unfolding sequences of moor, dale and scarp, as well as by spectacular individual features. The special scenic qualities of the landscape stem from the contrast between the extent, uniformity, simplicity, space and freedom of the moors, the enclosed, sheltered and domestic character of the dales and the drama of the scarp of the Vale of Eden.

The whole area is important as a historic mining landscape, and there is also exceptional importance attached to the unique flora and fauna, the unusual range of geological and geomorphological features and the wealth of archaeological and historical interest. Although less well known than other comparable upland areas, the qualities of the area have been recognised for many years, and an informed consensus has emerged that the landscape is of national importance. Our own landscape assessment leads us to agree wholeheartedly with that consensus.

Landscape types or areas that best demonstrate the special qualities of the North Pennines are Teesdale, the southern scarp, the high moorland summits and ridges, the lead areas of Weardale, South Tynedale, the Nent Valley, Rookhope, the two Allendales and the wooded gorges of lower Allendale and lower Derwentdale. Every part of the area has its own character and quality, from the most sheltered dale to the wildest moor. The North Pennines offer a landscape of contrasts and contradictions. As the inspector wrote in reaching his conclusion on AONB status:

> "We are in no doubt that the landscape in most of the area compares favourably with the scenery of a number of other AONBs with which we are familiar, and indeed also bears comparison with the scenery in some national parks. The remoteness and wild quality of the moorland, the dramatic contrast with the softer beauty of the dales, and the relief and the landscape shapes all combine to make the North Pennines in general terms an outstandingly beautiful area."

*The North Pennines offer many contrasts and contradictions, but few would dispute the outstanding qualities of the landscape.*

51

# References

1.  Countryside Commission, *Landscape assessment: A Countryside Commission approach*, CCD 18, 1987.

2.  Countryside Commission, *The Cambrian Mountains landscape*, CCP 293, 1990.

3.  Wallace, W, *Alston Moor – Its Pastoral People, its Mines and Miners*, Dans Books Ltd, Newcastle. First published 1890, reprinted 1986.

4.  Boyle, J R, *Leland the Antiquary in Durham and Northumberland*, The Monthly Chronicle of North Country Lore and Legend, Walter Scott Ltd, 1890.

5.  Hill, D, *In Turner's Footsteps*, John Murray Ltd, 1984.

6.  Hodgson, J, *History of Northumberland*, Part II, Vol. IV.

7.  Garland, R, *A Tour in Teesdale*, Whittaker and Co., 1804.

8.  Watson, R, *Poems and Songs of Teesdale*, William Dresser & Sons, 1930. (First edition 1862).

9.  Redfern, R A, *Portrait of The Pennines*, Robert Hale, 1969.

10. Wainwright, A, *Wainwright on The Pennine Way*, Michael Joseph Ltd., 1985.

11. Bellamy, D and Quayle B, *England's Last Wilderness: A Journey through the North Pennines*, Michael Joseph Ltd, 1989.

12. Boyle, J R, *The County of Durham – Its Castles, Churches and Manor Houses*, Walter Scott Ltd, 1892.

13. Bulmer, T F, *History, Topography and Directory of Cumberland*, 1901.

14. Egglestone, W, *Picturesque Weardale*, 1916.

15. Ramsden, D M, *Teesdale*, Museum Press, 1947.

16. Sopwith, T, *An Account of the Mining Districts of Alston Moor*, Alnwick, 1833.

17. Mitchell, W R, Pennine Lead-Miner, Eric Richardson, of Nenthead. *Personal Recollections of life in the North Pennines Orefield*, Dalesman Publishing Co. Ltd, 1979.

18. Mitchell, W R, *Wild Pennines*, Robert Hale, 1976.

19. Pennington, J, *British Countryside in Colour*, Odhams, 1950.

20. Hauxwell Hannah, with Cockcroft, Barry, *Seasons of my life – the Story of a Solitary Daleswoman*, Century Hutchinson, 1989.

21. Palmer, W J, *The Tyne and its Tributaries*, George Bell and Sons, 1882.

22. Spencer, B, *The Visitor's Guide to the Yorkshire Dales, Teesdale and Weardale*, Butler and Tanner Ltd, 1986.

23. Bellam, G A, *Rambles in the Derwent Valley – A Guide to Places of Interest and Beauty in the Derwent Valley*, Ramsden Williams, Consett, 1938 (2nd edition).

24. Proud, J K, *Weardale, Allendale and South Tynedale*, Discovery Guide, 1984.

25. Department of the Environment, North Pennines AONB (Designation) Order 1987, Public Local Inquiry – Inspector's Report, 1986.

26. Sinclair G. et al, *Upland Landscapes Study*, Lunedale Parish Report, unpublished study, 1979.

Brunskill, R W, *Vernacular Architecture of the Northern Pennines*, Northern History, Vol XI. pp 107-142, 1975.

Council for the Protection of Rural England, *England's Glory: A Photographic Journey through England's Threatened Landscapes*, Weidenfield and Nicolson, 1987.

Countryside Commission, *North Pennines AONB Public Inquiry, October 1985: Statement by G. Coggins*, 1985.

Countryside Commission, *The North Pennines AONB: Issues and priorities*, CCP 289, 1990.

Jacobs, M, and Warner, M, *The Phaidon Companion to Art and Artists in the British Isles*, Phaidon, 1980.

Raistrick, A, *The Pennine Dales*, Eyre & Spottiswoode Ltd., 1968.

# Acknowledgements

We would like to thank the following organisations and individuals who helped us in preparation of the report: Dr Peter Howard of Exeter College of Art and Design for assistance with research concerning art and literature; the staff of Durham, Northumberland and Cumbria County Councils for their comments on landscape history; the staff of the East Cumbria Countryside Project for their very helpful comments on the draft report; and last but not least, Shelagh Reynolds of the Countryside Commission's Northern Regional Office for her support and advice.

Land Use Consultant's project team was Carys Swanwick, Martin Tabor and Ric Eales. The watercolour illustrations are by Martin Tabor.

We are grateful to Simon Warner and Chris Buckley for the photographs.